AUTHORS

Paolo Crippa (23 April 1978) has cultivated his passion for Italian history since high school. His research interests are focused mainly in the field of military history and in particular on italian armored units from the 30s until the end of World War II. In 2006 he published his first volume, "I Reparti Corazzati della Repubblica Sociale Italiana 1943/1945", the first organic research carried out and published in Italy on the subject. In 2007 he published "Duecento Volti della R.S.I." and in 2011 " Un anno con il 27° Reggimento Artiglieria Legnano". He regularly contributes to several journals: Milites, New Historica, SGM - World War II, Batailes & Blindes, Armoured Vehicles and history of the twentieth century, Mezzi Corazzati, both as an author, or in collaboration with other researchers. He published with the editor Mattioli 1885 in 2014 "Italy 43 – 45 – Civil War improvised AFV's" (2014), "Italian AFV's of the Civil War 1943 - 1945" (2015) and "Italy 43 – 45 – AFV's and MV's of co-belligerent units" (2018).

Carlo Cucut was born in Nole (TO) in 1955. He cultivated a passion for history as a boy and over the years has deepened this interest by dedicating himself to historical research. He published articles in the italian magazines: "Storia del XX Secolo", "Storie & Battaglie", "Milites" and "Ritterkreuz". He published various volumes for Marvia Edizioni: "Penne Nere on the eastern border. History of the Alpini's Regiment "Tagliamento" 1943-1945 ", winner of the "De Cia" Award; "Attilio Viziano. Memories of a war correspondent "; "Armed Forces of RSI on the eastern front"; "Armed Forces of RSI on the Western Front"; "Armed Forces of RSI on the Gothic Line"; "Alpini in the City of Rijeka 1944-1945". For the Trentino Modeling Group he published "The armed forces of RSI 1943-1945. Land forces ".

PUBLISHING'S NOTES

None of unpublished images or text of our book may be reproduced in any format without the expressed written permission of Luca Cristini Editore (already Soldiershop.com) when not indicate as marked with license creative commons 3.0 or 4.0. Luca Cristini Editore has made every reasonable effort to locate, contact and acknowledge rights holders and to correctly apply terms and conditions to Content.
Every effort has been made to trace the copyright of all the photographs. If there are unintentional omissions, please contact the publisher in writing at: info@soldiershop.com, who will correct all subsequent editions.
Our trademark: Luca Cristini Editore@, and the names of our series & brand: Soldiershop, Witness to war, Museum book, Bookmoon, Soldiers&Weapons, Battlefield, War in colour, Historical Biographies, Darwin's view, Fabula, Altrastoria, Italia Storica Ebook, Witness To History, Soldiers, Weapons & Uniforms, Storia etc. are herein @ by Luca Cristini Editore.

LICENSES COMMONS

This book may utilize part of material marked with license creative commons 3.0 or 4.0 (CC BY 4.0), (CC BY-ND 4.0), (CC BY-SA 4.0) or (CC0 1.0). We give appropriate attribution credit and indicate if change were made in the acknowledgments field. Our WTW books series utilize only fonts licensed under the SIL Open Font License or other free use license.

For a complete list of Soldiershop titles please contact Luca Cristini Editore on our website: www.soldiershop.com or www.cristinieditore.com. E-mail: info@soldiershop.com

Title: **M.D.T. - TERRITORIAL DEFENSE MILITIA AND CIVIC GUARDS IN THE O.Z.A.K. 1943-1945** Code.: **WTW-008 EN**
By Carlo Cucut and Paolo Crippa.
ISBN code: 978-88-93275507 first edition February 2020
Language: English, Nr. of images: 87, Size: 177,8x254mm, Cover & Art Design: Luca S. Cristini

WITNESS TO WAR (SOLDIERSHOP) is a trademark of Luca Cristini Editore, via Orio, 35/4 - 24050 Zanica (BG) ITALY.

WITNESS TO WAR

M.D.T. - TERRITORIAL DEFENSE MILITIA AND CIVIC GUARDS IN THE O.Z.A.K. 1943-1945

PHOTOS & IMAGES FROM WORLD WARTIME ARCHIVES

PAOLO CRIPPA - CARLO CUCUT

BOOKS TO COLLECT

SUMMARY

OPERATIONSZONE ADRIATISCHES KUSTENLAND O.Z.A.K. ....Pag. 5

TERRITORIAL DEFENSE MILITIA .... Pag. 7

    Territorial Defense Militia Headquarter..Pag. 8

    Special O.P. Battalion of Trieste..Pag. 9

    1st Regiment M.D.T. (58th Legion) "San Giusto"............................ Pag. 17

    2nd Regiment M.D.T. (60th Legion) "Istria"..................................... Pag. 23

    "Mazza di Ferro" Company.. Pag. 36

    3rd Regiment M.D.T. (61st Legion) "Carnaro"................................ Pag. 43

    4th Regiment M.D.T. (62nd Legion) "Gorizia"................................ Pag. 57

    5th Regiment M.D.T. (63rd Legion) "Friuli".................................... Pag. 62

    S.A.F. Preparation Center.. Pag. 64

    M.D.T. Confinaria (Frontier)... Pag. 65

    M.D.T. Specials.. Pag. 65

    Armaments and uniforms of the M.D.T.. Pag. 66

CIVIC GUARDS IN THE O.Z.A.K..Pag. 77

    Trieste's Civic Guard...Pag. 78

    Gorizia's Civic Guard..Pag. 81

    Koper's Civic Guard..Pag. 82

    Pordenone's civic guard..Pag. 84

Bibliography .... Pag. 96

OPERATIONSZONE ADRIATISCHES KUSTENLAND – O.Z.A.K.

With the proclamation of the Armistice, Italy remained divided into two: the few Southern Regions, already under the control of the Allied forces, where the King and Marshal Badoglio had taken refuge, and most of the North - Central area, which was preparing to be divided into two zones under German control, an Operations Zone under the control of Marshal Rommel and an Occupation Zone under the German Military Command. As of September 10th, the whole territory that includes the Friuli-Venezia Giulia, the Province of Ljubljana and Istria, considered vital for communication lines and for the supply of the German army in Italy, was placed, on the direct order of the Fuhrer, under the jurisdiction of the Gauleiter Friedrick Alois Rainer. It was only the first step towards the creation of the O.Z.A.K. (Operationszone Adriatisches Kustenland - Zone of Operations of the Adriatic Coast). In fact, with this move, the Germans intended to expel these territories from Italian sovereignty and proceed subsequently to their incorporation into Austria and therefore to the Reich. With the establishment of the Italian Social Republic, the new Republican government sought to maintain jurisdiction over those Italic lands conquered with the sacrifice of thousands of Italian soldiers during the First World War: the clash between Italian authorities and O.Z.A.K. authorities, clearly pro-Austrian it was long and violent. In all fields, the Gauleiter Rainer tried, almost always succeeding, to impose his directives, even if in some cases he had to withdraw, for example, the case of the Administration of Justice, where the Friulian Minister Piero Pisenti managed to the Italian Code was maintained. Rainer's closed, wary and provocative attitude also clashed with the local Italian military leaders, while the relations of the Italians with the leaders of the Wehrmacht were based on maximum collaboration. In fact, there was a division of tasks in the military: the struggle against the Italian and Slav partisans was the responsibility of the Political-military Security Structure, essentially of the SS, while the coastal and front-line defense was pertaining to the Wehrmacht LXXXXVII Armeekorps. This dualism was the source of tactical errors during the fight against the Tito's partisans, of failure to promptly support the Italian units heavily engaged in combat, of a lack of information of a tactical and strategic nature that could have improved the course anti-partisan operations, the scarce supply of adequate armaments and materials to improve the defensive positions to the Italian units, in short, of many situations that caused heavy losses among the Italian units deployed in the numerous defensive positions in the Adriatic Coast. Voluntary membership of fascist militias was the only form of armed collaboration that the Germanic Command allowed. In fact, when the government of the R.S.I. also tried to organize in the O.Z.A.K. units called to the draft, was ordered by the Germans to immediately revoke any provision, so much so that, to inform citizens also of these directives, an order from Commissioner Rainer was published in the Trieste newspaper "Il Piccolo" which stressed that "[...] recalls and enlistments in the Adriatic coast can only take place on a voluntary basis". A few months later, on March 8th, 1944, it was Rainer himself who signed the decree for compulsory mobilization for young people of the classes 1923, 1924 and 1925, because the Germans needed the collaboration of Italian elements for the so-called " territorial defense ", that is the repression of the partisan phenomenon.

---

1 "Il Piccolo", November 11th, 1943.

The announcement imposed the choice to be enrolled in the T.O.D.T. Organization or in the units of the Social Republic, and the majority, precisely in order not to expose themselves politically, chose forced labor. However, an escape route was offered by the establishment of the Civic Guard in Trieste, a self-defense unit promoted by the Prefect Coceani and the Podestà Pagnini.

On June 22nd, 1944, an order of the Major General of the SS Mundhenke forbade "all troops and dependent Command Departments from hoisting flags and pennants of their national colors", effectively preventing the display of the tricolor flag.

Mussolini himself, concerned about the growing denationalization of Venezia Giulia and Istria, in favor of a pro-Austrian and pro-German policy, sent the Secretary of the Republican Fascist Party and Minister Secretary of State Alessandro Pavolini in January 1945 to visit these lands, stolen de facto from the authority of the Italian Social Republic. Pavolini went to Udine, Gorizia, Fiume, Trieste and talked to the representatives of the Republican Fascist Party, of which he collected complaints about the bulky German ally who favored the Croatian element at the expense of the Italians. In Trieste, where he gave a speech based on the defense of the Italian spirit of the city at the "Verdi" Theater in Trieste, Pavolini was received by the High Commissioner Rainer, but only as Secretary of the P.F.R. and not as Minister of the R.S.I., as a sign of contempt for the republican authority. Once he arrived at the gates of Pula, the German authorities even prevented him from visiting the city, citing empty military reasons.

By hindering the work of the Italian Commands in every way, effectively relegating them to a pure administrative activity, hindering visits to the units of local Commanders, trying in every way to sever any contact with the Government of R.S.I., creating a situation of opposition between the Wehrmacht and the SS on the management of the Italian units, facilitating the presence on the Italian territory of the Slovenian and Croatian collaborative formations, which often risked to enter into conflict with our military, and by exauthoring those commanders who tried to hinder his pro-Austrian policy, Rainer obtained the result of not allowing that overview that would have allowed the Italian units to better defend the eastern border from Tito's annexation aims, thus creating the tragic presupposition for the epilogue experienced by the populations of Friuli-Venezia Giulia and Istria during the Slavic occupation of May 1945, the tragedy of the foibe and that of the hundreds of Italians who disappeared into thin air.

Operationszone Adriatisches Kustenland

Jurisdiction: Provinces of Udine, Gorizia, Trieste, Pola, Fiume, Ljubljana, Kvarner, territories of Sussak, Buccari, Cabar, Castua, island of Veglia.
Supreme Commissioner: Doctor Friedrich Rainer
Political-military structure for security:
• Commander: SS-Gruppenfüher Odilo Globocnik
• Chief of staff: Sturmbannfuher Ernst Lerch
• Wehrmacht: LXXXXVII Armeekorps (97th Mountain Army Corp) - Commander: General Ludwig Kubler
Kriegsmarine: Admiral Kommando "Adria"

M.D.T. TERRITORIAL DEFENSE MILITIA

Following the order for the establishment of the O.Z.A.K., the Provinces of Trieste, Gorizia, Udine, Pola, Istria, Kvarner and Fiume passed under the management of the German Administration. Among the many consequences of this ordinance, and therefore of the interference of the SS and other German military bodies, there was also opposition to the birth of a Militia that was not intended if not as "Landschutz", that is a defense unit of the territory. Immediately after the Armistice in the Julian regions the local Legions of the M.V.S.N. had been reconstituted, at the Deposits and the Territorial Commands, gathering around the old "squadristi", to the Black Shirts returned from the different fronts, to the young volunteers who had not accepted the Armistice and to those who recognized themselves in the new republican fascism. The main activity of these formations was the maintenance of public order and the fight against the partisan movement. With Legislative Decree No. 913 of the Duce on 24 December 1943, with the effect backdated to 20th November, the Republican National Guard was formed, the military formation which incorporated the specialties of the Militia, the Carabinieri and the P.A.I., with the task of:

1) ensure internal order
2) enforce the laws of the Italian Social Republic
3) ensure the orderly conduct of all manifestations of national life.

Even the Legions of the Militia present in the Adriatic Coast should have adopted this name, becoming part of the new body. The German authorities, with the intention of excluding any form of influence from the R.S.I. in the OZAK territory, on the other hand, they prohibited the use of the denomination Republican National Guard in the region, used only a few months between the end of 1943 and the beginning of 1944, but, after not easy negotiations, imposed the formations of the Militia on the denomination of Territorial Defense Militia (M.D.T.), formally part of the G.N.R., but in the autonomous reality.

The General Command of the G.N.R. taking note of the situation, issued a circular in May 1944 in which it ordered the transformation of M.V.S.N. in the O.Z.A.K. in M.D.T., instituted a Superior Command of the M.D.T. of the Adriatic Coast and ordered the 5 Militia Legions present in the region to take on the new name of the Territorial Defense Militia Regiment, in fact the literal translation of the German name "Landschutz", with which the Militia units were continued to be identified. This imposition on the name was badly accepted by the members of the units, although having kept the reference to the Legions alongside the new name made the situation more acceptable.

M.V.S.N. Legions organization chart (September - December 1943)

• Headquarter of 6th Zone CC.NN. - Commander: Consul General Aristide Chiappa, later Italian Consul General Di Pasquale

• 55th Legion "Alpina Friulana" in Gemona

• 58th Legion "San Giusto" in Trieste

• 59th Legion "Carso" in (later absorbed by 58th Legion)

• 60th Legion "Istria" in Pola

• 61st Legion "Carnaro" in Fiume

• 62nd Legion "Isonzo" in Gorizia

• 63rd Legion "Tagliamento" in Udine

M.D.T. organization chart (since december 1943)
- Headquarter (Trieste)
- 1st Regiment (58th Legion) "San Giusto"
- 2nd Regiment (60th Legion) "Istria"
- 3rd Regiment (61st Legion) "Fiume"
- 4th Regiment (62nd Legion) "Gorizia"
- 5th Regiment (63rd Legion) "Udine"[2]
- M.D.T. Confinaria (1 Battalion and 3 Autonomous Companies)
- M.D.T. Specialities:
  - M.D.T. Postelegrafonica
  - M.D.T. Forestale
  - M.D.T. Ferroviaria
  - M.D.T. Portuaria
  - M.D.T. Stradale

Each regiment of the M.D.T. had a German police officer who acted as a liaison with the Ordnungspolizei in Trieste and as an operational guide and from his own Political Investigation Office (U.P.I.), who collected information regarding the actions, the elements and the location of the partisan brigades. The Territorial Defense Militia, including its Specialties, reached a total strength of 10,144 men.

Territorial Defense Militia Headquarter
After Mussolini's arrest, the Command of the VI Black Shirts Zone of Trieste was ruled by General Lorenzo Mugnati of the Royal Army. With the Armistice and the subsequent German occupation of the city, the command was transferred to the Italian Consul General Di Pasquale until January 28, 1944, subsequently replaced by Major General Ambrogio Battiston[3] and finally it was ruled by the Consul General (later Major General) Angelo Sommavilla[4].
With the birth of the Territorial Defense Militia, the Command of the VI Zone Camice Nere changed its name first, for a short time, to the Inspectorate of the Territorial Defense Militia and then took the definitive name of the Superior Command Territorial Defense Militia, on which the Regiments depended and the Special Militias.
Due to the firm opposition of the German authorities to establish Italian Grand Units in the O.Z.A.K., The Command never carried out operational tasks and was relegated to purely bureaucratic tasks. It was therefore not possible to transform the body of the M.D.T. in a real organic Division and the decision-making power was, in fact, the German military commands.
On 20th November 1944 General Angelo Sommavilla, Commander of the Territorial Defense

---
2 Altogether the 5 Regiments consisted of 14 Battalions and 3 Autonomous Companies.
3 According to Stefano Di Giusto it is instead the Major General Augusto Bastianon.
4 According to some sources, also the following departments also depended from the Superior Command of the M.D.T.:
- Training Company (actually dependent on the 2nd Regiment)
- Officers and Petty Officers School (actually dependent on the 2nd Regiment)
- Complements Battalion (actually dependent on the 2nd Regiment)5th Italian Police Battalion in Gorizia
- Civic Guard of Trieste
- Civic Guard of Gorizia
- Special Services Battalion in Udine, formed by the Carabinieri (who was actually part of the 5th Regiment).

Militia, was received at the Headquarters in Gargnano, at Villa Orsoline by Benito Mussolini. Sommavilla was accompanied by Lieutenant Colonel Giuseppe Porcu, Commander of the 3rd M.D.T. "Carnaro", by Colonel Attilio De Lorenzi, Commander of the 5th M.D.T. Regiment "Friuli", and by Major Gualtiero Plisca, Commander of the 1st "San Giusto" Regiment. The latter gave Mussolini a document containing a long report on the activity carried out by the 1st Regiment, while De Lorenzi and Porcu gave the Duce parchment memories of the 61st "Gabriele d'Annunzio" Legion of Fiume and of the 63rd "Tagliamento" Legion of Udine, progenitors of the respective Militia Regiments.

At the end of April the Command retreated towards the Tarvisio pass, reaching the lower Isonzo on April 30th, 1945, where the 1st M.D.T.Regiment had also met, and broke up on the same day.

Special O.P. Battalion of Trieste

This Battalion was the forerunner of the Regiments of the M.D.T., in which all its members came together in the spring of 1944. The Battalion originated from the 137th Black Shirt Assault Legion, consisting of the 137th and the 134th Black Shirt Battalion, which it was in Croatia at the time of the Armistice, employed by the "Lombardy" Division. At the news of the Armistice, the "Lombardy" Division dropped arms, while the 137th Legion CC.NN., determined to continue the fight, began a march of retreat through Slovenia, up to San Pietro del Carso, where the Black Shirts were taken over as prisoners by the local German garrison. After being transferred to a barracks in Postojna, crowded with disbanded Italian soldiers waiting for their fate, the Legionaries, led by Captain Giovanni Downie, asked the German authorities to be able to resume fighting under the banner of R.S.I., which in the meantime had been made up. The Legionaries were thus transferred to Trieste at the headquarters of the 58th Legion, where their rearmament was carried out, first constituting the Special Battalion "S. Giusto". The unit thus formed already in September with the young volunteers who rushed there, was hosted in the barracks "Vittorio Emanuele III" in via Rossetti, renamed "Ettore Muti". The huge building, which had housed the "Sassari" Brigade, remained empty and the volunteers who came to it found numerous empty dormitories available.

An elderly officer from Pula, Lieutenant Romano Baxa, was sent to command the unit, who had the task of giving the boys some military spirit. The newly established Special Battalion O.P. (Public Order) of Trieste was organized on:

- Headquarter
- 1st Rifle Company (in Trieste)
- 2nd Rifle Company (in Parenzo, Visignano, Mompaderno)
- 3rd Rifle Company (in Lupogliano, Lanischie, Baetto)
- 4th Rifle Company (in Assia)
- 5th Rifle Company (in Buie, Umago, Visinada)
- 6th Rifle Company (in Pinguente)
- 7th Machine Guns Company (in support to the diffent Companies)

The command was initially entrusted to Maggiore Filtri, who was replaced by Lieutenant Colonel Rossetti and, finally, Maggiore Roman. The departments were armed with Italian weapons, 91 muskets and 45mm Brixia light mortars.

The 5th Rifle Company, commanded by Captain Downie, the true promoter of the birth of the department, was the first to reach maximum efficiency and it paraded through the streets of Trieste to demonstrate to the population, strongly proven by the German presence and the titin pressure, that an Italian Army was being reorganized in defense of Venezia Giulia. The Company of Captain Downie was the only unit to participate in the "Cloudburst" Operation[5], entering Buje on 4th October, Umag on 5th and, in the following days, proceeding with the liberation from the Slavic militias in Mompaderno, Visinada, Visignano and Parenzo, establishing garrisons to defend the population in every locality. In some of these locations, such as Pazin, Portole, Levade, Montona Santo Stefano and Piran, citizens voluntarily formed small militias, which operated for a short time in support of the activity of the 5th Company.

In the following weeks of October, as many as 5 Battalion's Companies were employed between Trieste and Gorizia to guard the area and the communication routes, after the vast German operation "Cloudburst" had driven away bands of Slav partisans from Istria. During this cycle of operations, on 7th October, Giuseppe Cossetto was assassinated, who was attached to the 5th Company. Giuseppe was the father of the sadly famous Norma Cossetto, a young student from Visinada (in Istria), kidnapped by the titian partisans after the Armistice, in retaliation against the family and especially against his father, local leader of the National Fascist Party. Norma's father, who left the ward to go looking for his daughter, fell into an ambush strained by the partisans, unaware that the girl had already been brutally tortured by the Slavs and thrown alive in a foiba near Pazin.

The Battalion detachments controlled the Istrian region throughout the winter of 1943 - '44, containing as far as possible the presence of the Slav partisans and allowing to proceed with the recovery of the remains of the Italians thrown into the sinkholes between September and October 1943.

At the beginning of February, the Battalion's Companies were hit by a Slavic offensive, which was soon rejected. The biggest losses occurred on day 2nd, when a column, made up of 46 soldiers from the Battalion O.P. and 34 Polizei soldiers, aboard 8 trucks and an armored car, were signaled by a powerful attack of partisans, also supported by anti-tank guns, near Rifembergo (Gorizia). At the end of the tremendous fight, which lasted 5 hours, all the Republican and German soldiers lay dead on the field, with the exception of a single Italian survivor, who escaped although wounded. A relief column of SS-Karstwher Bataillon, sent by Gradisca d'Isonzo, arrived too late and could only ascertain the extent of the massacre.

In the spring of 1944, the Special Battalion O.P. was dissolved, following an organic reorganization, following the establishment of the Territorial Defense Militia, and its Companies merged into the 1st Militia Regiment.

---

[5] Operation "Cloudburst" ("Wolkenbruch") was a large-scale German military offensive, which began on October 2nd, 1943. With the aim of taking control of Venezia Giulia, the province of Ljubljana and Istria, which had been occupied by the Yugoslav partisans after the Armistice. Under the command of SS General Paul Hausser, the SS-Division "Leibstandarte SS Adolf Hitler", the 7. SS-Gebirgsdivision "Prinz Eugen", unit of the 162. Turkmenische Infanterie-Division, the 24. Panzer-Division, the 44. Reichs-Grenadierdivision and 71. Infanterie-Division, as well as reduced recently reconstituted fascist units, including the 5th Company of the Special O.P. Battalion of Trieste. The troops entered Istria on three columns, after strong preparatory bombardments, annihilating the partisan departments who retreated inside. Resistance cores tried to slow down the Germans, who reacted by hitting the civilian population, also of Italian ethnicity, with indiscriminate shootings, violence, village fires and looting. The "Wolkenbruch" operation ended on October 9th with the conquest of Rovinj. The systematic mopping up of Istria went on, however throughout the month of October and not only the partisan movement, but above all civilians, both Italian and Slavic, were brutally affected, causing about 2,500 victims.

▲ The Operational Zone of the Adriatic Coast or O.Z.A.K. (acronym for "Operationszone Adriatisches Küstenland") included the Italian provinces of Udine, Gorizia, Trieste, Pola, Fiume and Ljubljana, subject to direct German military administration and therefore effectively removed from the control of the Italian Social Republic.

M.D.T. ORGANIZATION CHART

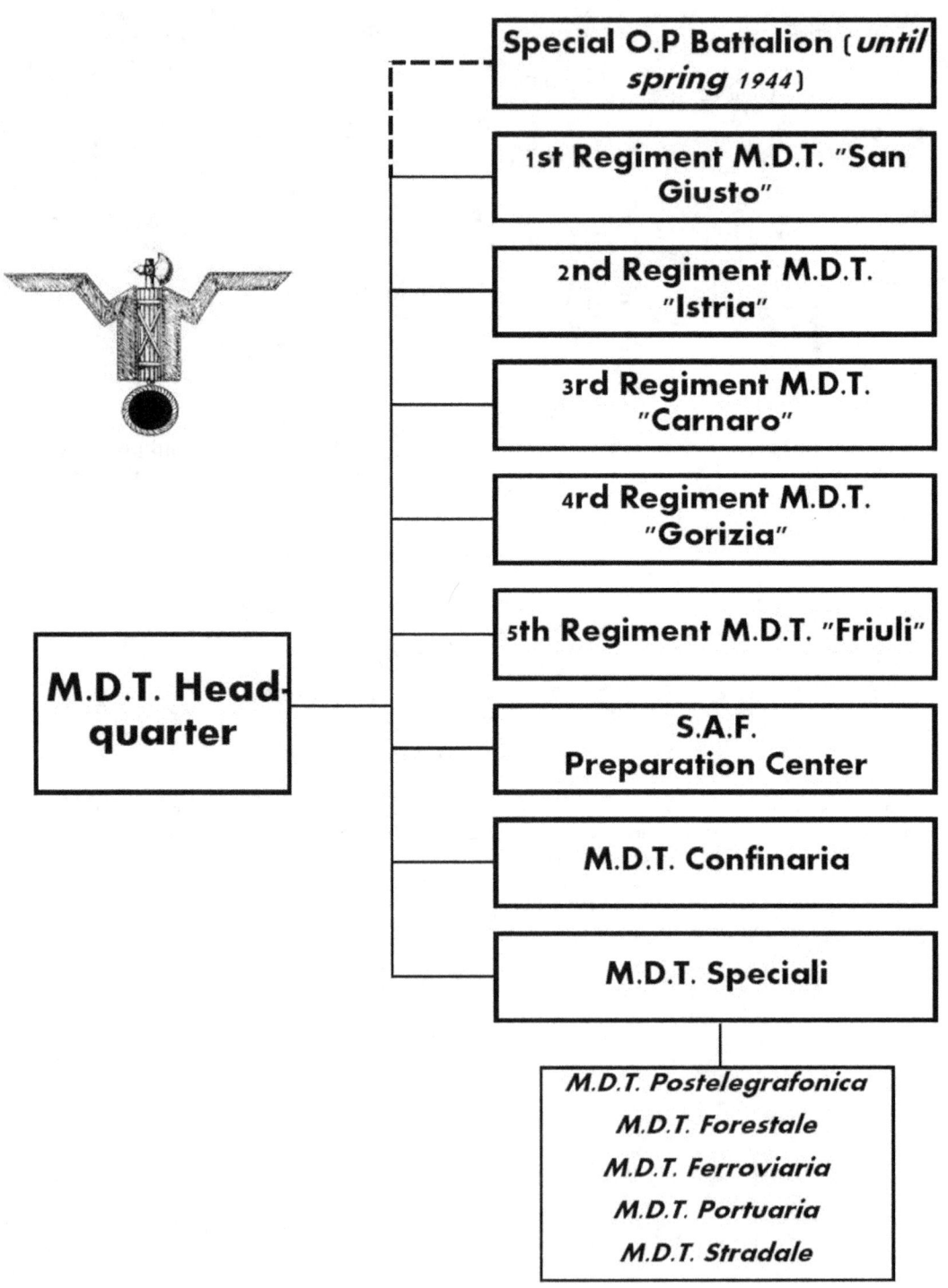

▲ On April 20th, 1944, the German authorities organized a spectacular military parade in Trieste, on the occasion of the birthday of Adolf Hitler, which saw the mass participation of the German Armed Forces, as a show of strength also against the Italian population. On the stage of the authorities we find, from the left, the SS-Gruppenfüher Odilo Globocnik, the Supreme Commissioner of the O.Z.A.K. Dr. Friedrich Rainer, General Ludwig Kubler and General Harry Hoppe (Adria Illustrierte).

▼ Another image of the Trieste parade, which ended with the concentration of all the units in front of the city's Palace of Justice. The Italian participation was absolutely marginal. A similar event also took place simultaneously in Ljubljana (Adria Illustrierte).

▲ An SS department on the seafront in Trieste parades in front of the German military authorities. (Adria Ilustrierte).

▼ A unit of the R.S.I. parades in front of Globoknik and Kubler (Adria Illustrierte).

▲ A legionnaire of the newly reconstituted Militia in Venezia Giulia fraternizes with a German soldier (Arena)

▼ Soldiers of the newly reconstituted Militia in comradeship with German soldiers: some of them come from the "M" Battalions.

▲ The Black Shirts of the 137th Assault Legion CC.NN. after the Armistice decided to continue the war alongside the German Armed Forces. After a troubled period, opposed by the Germans themselves, they managed to organize a Battalion O.P. in the city of Trieste (Arena).

▶ The final concentration of troops in front of the Palace of Justice in Trieste. No tricolour flag is displayed, in defiance of the Italian spirit of the region: only a small coat of arms of the municipality of Trieste appears on a column of the palace (Adria Illustrierte).

1st Regiment M.D.T. (58th Legion) "San Giusto"

The 1st "San Giusto" Regiment originated from the mobilization headquarters of the 58th Legion CC.NN. "San Giusto" and, for the rest, from the CXXXIV Assault Battalion CC.NN., which had returned from eastern Slovenia in perfect working order, and by the 137th Assault Legion CC.NN. which, as we have seen, at the Armistice had refused to give up its arms to the Titines, as done by the G.U., and had opened the way to Slovenia, where it had been stopped by the Germans[6]. Transferred to Trieste, they proceeded to their rearmament, first forming the Special Battalion "S. Giusto" then, with the arrival of new volunteers and legionaries, the other departments.

The operational activity then began and ended only with the end of the conflict. The activity carried out by the Departments of the 1st M.D.T. "San Giusto" was that of garrison and control of the territory, repression of crime, fight against partisan gangs, defense of infrastructures from attacks and sabotages; activity carried out with the formation of principals and cornerstones, with raking and counter-guerrilla actions.

The first actions carried out were essentially directed in two directions. The first was to escort the vehicles that brought the soldiers to reopen the barracks and garrisons in Istria, which had just been freed from the Tito gangs by the German wards in early October. Traveling the Istrian streets in those days meant seeing rows of partisans with the red star at the edges of the roads at every step. They were those who had tried to counter, but had been swept away, the advance of the German units supported by armored vehicles, but also those who had begun to fill the sinkholes of Istria with many Italians. The population, seeing again soldiers who wore gray-green uniforms, applauded and comforted them with total support, it was Italy that was returning. The other direction was to create and then supply the garrisons in the Karst north of Trieste, in particular in Comeno and Rifembergo. Elderly soldiers, war experts, were sent to the garrisons, while the young and inexperienced legionaries had the task of escorting the columns that brought food and ammunition to those cornerstones[7].

Particularly difficult was the situation of the various garrisons and cornerstones, systematically subject to daytime and nighttime attacks, carried out by partisan formations much more consistent than the defenders and with considerable firepower, difficult to supply, given that the supply columns were always at risk of ambushes, frequently isolated for the encirclement by rebel formations and unable to request and obtain the necessary help which meant salvation. There are dozens and dozens of episodes that involved all the places where the soldiers of the "San Giusto" were present, just as countless were the gunfights during control actions carried out on the territory.

The investigation carried out by the U.P.I. was extremely important and by the Regimental Departments, which led to the capture of many members of the Communist, Italian and Slavic formations, perpetrators of crimes, attacks and sabotages in the various localities of the Province and in the city of Trieste itself.

The "San Giusto" departments also participated in mopping up actions, in collaboration with

---

6 See the previous chapter "Special O.P. Battalion of Trieste"
7 We transcribe the testimony of a veteran of the Department, Claudio de Ferra: *"After loading the material to Opicina, we arrived on those treacherous roads where we could see partisan expectations among the woods. In front of the garrison of Rifembergo there was every time a beautiful collection of unexploded hand grenades, machine gun shells, mortar splinters. Chills came. The soldiers were there to watch us as dying and we to them: "Ah, you breathe in the day, but hell at night. They come under assaulting the garrison and then in the morning they take away their dead and wounded. I don't know how long it will last before we are all killed." On our return every time we thanked the Madonna who had saved us."*

other departments of the M.D.T. and Germans, and to protect the workers engaged in the repair of road and railway works damaged by the actions of the partisans.

The most serious episode, which struck the 1st "San Giusto" Regiment, occurred on February 2, 1944, when the 1st Battalion's truck, which carried supplies and reinforcements to the Rifembergo garrison, fell into an ambush during of which 46 legionnaires were killed. The truck, which left Trieste and consisted of 8 trucks and a self-protected, under the command of Captain Costantini and Lieutenant Mombelli, had the task of supplying the garrisons of Comeno and Rifembergo. In Comeno a group of 36 German soldiers with 4 trucks, headed on the same route, and 11 other legionaries had joined the column. When the column arrived about 5 km from Rifembergo, near a curve between two lateral woods, the road was found to be barred and was suddenly taken under the crossfire of dozens of automatic weapons. After 5 hours of fire, the ammunition ran out and with most of the men killed, the reaction stopped and the partisans came out into the open to finish the wounded. After stripping the bodies and recovering the weapons, the corpses were loaded onto the lorry platforms and the whole column was set on fire. When the reinforcements arrived, it was only possible to proceed to the pitiful recovery of the corpses and to rescue the only survivor, seriously injured, left alive because he thought he was dead. In total 46 Italians and 39 Germans died, but the bodies of 11 legionaries were never recovered.

The 1st "San Giusto" Regiment ceased to exist between 29 and 30 April 1945 in the lower Isonzo and Carnia area.

Organization chart 1st Regiment "San Giusto"

- Headquarter (Trieste)
    - Commander: Consul Angelo Sommavilla subsequently the Lieutenant Colonel Gualtiero Plisca
    - Major Adjutant: Major Mingotti
    - Chaplain Officer: Lieutenant Epaminonda Don Troja
    - "P" Officer: Captain Giovanni Posabella
- Verbindungsoffizier: Hauptmann Strauch
- U.P.I. (Political Investigation Office) - Commander: Captain Corallo, later Captain Luigi Paraspin
- S.A.F. Nucleous (Women Auxiliary Service)- Commander: Auxiliary Gemma de Calò
- 1st Battalion – Commander: Major Giuseppe De Guarino
    - 1st Company
    - 2nd Company
    - 3rd Company
- 2nd Battalion – Commander: Major Giovanni Downie, later Captain Giovanni Posabella finally Capitano Aldo Bampi
    - 4th Company - Commander: Captain Spanghero
    - 5th Company - Commander: Captain Arcieri
    - 6th Company - Commander: Captain de Cristoforis
    - 7th Company - Commander: Captain Posi

- 3rd Special O.P. Battalion (later dissolved) - Commander: Major Tullio Filtri, later Lieutenant Colonel Luigi Rossetti

The Regiment had jurisdiction over a large part of the province of Trieste, with Battalion Commands located between Trieste and Pieris, with thirty garrisons, some also in the Gorizia area, assigned to control the Trieste-Pola-Fiume, Trieste-Postumia and Trieste- railways. Monfalcone-Gorizia, roads of great communication, important works and artifacts, civil and military installations. The Company Commands were in: Ronchi dei Legionari, Monrupino, Monfalcone, Comeno, Rifembergo and with a mobile department in Gorizia. In addition, garrisons had been organized in San Dorligo della Valle, Castel Lupogliano, Muggia, Gattinara, Longera, Sant'Antonio in Bosco, Bagnoli, Ceserano, Prebenico, Plava, Monte Castellier, Monte Guerca, Villa Opicina, Trieste, Comeno, Erpelle, Villa Decani, Buzet, Monfalcone, San Quirico di Buzet, Aurisina, Cave Auremiane, Lesecce, Divaccia, Draga, Sant'Elia, Moccò, Sesana and Gabrovizza. The regiment in December 1943 had a staff of 1,337 men, divided between 55 officers, 172 non-commissioned officers and 1,120 soldiers. In February 1945 there were 48 officers and 934 non-commissioned officers and soldiers for the 1st San Giusto Regiment.

Losses

In December 1944, the regimental casualties exceeded a hundred men and in total, at the date of the dissolution at the end of April 1945, the confirmed casualties were 324.

▲ On November 13th, 1943 in the main square of Koper, in front of the Pretorio Palace, a demonstration was held in support of the Republican Armed Forces, with the intent to encourage the voluntarism of the inhabitants of the area, in which some armored trucks participated. It is the very first photographic evidence of the presence of armored vehicles of the "Mazza di Ferro" Company of the reconstituted Militia (MNZ).

▲ In another image of the demonstration of the previous photo, it is noted that one of the soldiers aboard an armored FIAT 626 holds up a flag with the inscription "Iron Mace". The vehicle bears a showy camouflage with large green and brown spots on a yellow sand background and, on the front door, a large number "1", painted in white, the meaning of which is not known (MNZ).

▼ German and Italian military authorities review a unit of the reconstituted Militia in Venezia Giulia (Arena).

▲ A legionnaire of the newly reconstituted Militia in Istria after the Armistice (Arena).

▲ On February 2nd, 1944 an Italian - German column was attacked by Slav partisans near Rifembergo. After a long fight all the soldiers were killed, and all the vehicles set on fire. In the photo, a Fiat 665 Protetto truck, probably from the Battalion O.P. Trieste, destroyed by fire (MNZ).

▼ Another image taken after the massacre of Italian and German soldiers in Rifembergo. Only one Italian soldier managed to miraculously escape death.

2nd Regiment M.D.T. (60th Legion) "Istria"

The 2nd "Istria" Regiment was formed by the commander Libero Sauro, son of the hero Nazario, former naval officer as his father, and subsequently classified in the Voluntary National Security Militia. The regiment arose on the remains of the 60th Legion CC.NN. "Istria", in whose mobilization site, after the Armistice, 14 officers, 25 non-commissioned officers and 146 elderly legionaries, reinforced by 48 volunteers, remained in arms. On this basis, by bringing together all the groups of volunteers that had sprung up everywhere in Istria, in late November the commander Sauro formed the Volunteer Regiment "Istria", then merged into the GNR, managing in a short time to form 2 Battalions (which became 3 in 1945), the "Tramontana" Autonomous Company located on the island of Cres, the "Mazza di Ferro" Mobile Company and CAM, Military Training Center.

The war activity of the 2nd M.D.T. "Istria" began immediately after its formation, with the establishment of garrisons in the places to be protected, the construction of the necessary defensive works, the control and surveillance of the territory. The Regiment also opposed the interference of the German authorities, who sought to undermine the feelings of Italianness of the inhabitants of the region and played a fundamental role in maintaining public order con the support of the Carabinieri, who in OZ.A.K. they had not been incorporated into the Territorial Defense Militia[8].

The first clashes began immediately in the localities of Gallesano, Marzana, Porec, Koper, Rovinj, Arsia, with the first legionnaires who fell under Slavic fire. The attacks on the supply columns and on the garrisons scattered throughout Istria were numerous and bloody, many carried by the partisans of the Italian "Budicin" Battalion.

The intensity of the clashes, detected by the monthly chronological sequence, had a resurgence starting from the month of January 1944, a list that, despite the arid data of the figures, allows us to glimpse what was the situation experienced by the soldiers and what were the consequences in terms of human losses: in January 4 clashes, 13 in February, 22 in March, 20 in April, 54 in May, 34 in June, 21 in July, 16 in August, 22 in September, 23 in October, 7 in November, 14 in December. There is no data relating to the fighting sustained by the constitution until December 1943, because the department's documentation was destroyed following an air raid on January 19th, 1945.

Among the main attacks on the garrisons, we want to remember that of 13th June in Santa Domenica d'Albona, where 22 soldiers, under the command of Lieutenant Apollonio, attacked by about 400 partisans of the "Gortan" Brigade, resisted until they had run out of ammunition, At the end of the clash, while the survivors were translated as prisoners to Lizzul, the Lieutenant Apollonius, after being tortured, was killed with a barrage of machine guns. In an attempt to free the garrison of Santa Domenica d'Albona, the Regiment lost dozens more men between dead and wounded. On 30th June 1944 the garrison of Santo Stefano di Portole was invested, which was placed to guard the lifting water station.

---

[8] In the rest of the country the Carabinieri were incorporated into the structure of the Republican National Guard, effectively losing their autonomy.

After running out of ammunition and losing five fellow soldiers, the legionaries surrendered and the survivors were stabbed, except for two legionaries who managed to escape. In August the garrisons of Arsia and Pozzo Littorio, rejected with heavy losses, and the garrison of Visinada three times were made a sign of partisan attacks, on 6th, 12th and 26th August in Visinada, he had to repel the attackers titine, with a strong reaction. In the same month, the garrisons of Marzana, Roveria, Portole, Vrsar also faced enemy blitzes, which were also rejected thanks to the help of the local self-defense Auxiliary Militia.

In November, the partisan battalion "Alma Vivoda" was located and surrounded in the area of Toppolo di Dragogna by Italian-German forces, which was completely annihilated, after hard clashes, with the capture of a hundred partisans.

The escort to the autocolumns, responsible for the supply of the garrisons and civilians, was another of the main activities of the Departments of the "Istria" Regiment, with, also in this case, a very high number of ambushes and, in many cases, destruction of individuals means or of the column itself, with numerous losses in men and means. The Regiment's mobile departments participated in wide-ranging mopping-up actions and, in competition with the German troops, also in real war operations throughout Istria.

If this was the situation in Istria, the situation on the island of Cres and Losinj was not different, isolated and with little connection to the Regiment. On August 10th the British of S.B.S. (Special Boats Service) began a series of attacks on the garrisons of Cres and Lošinj, landing dozens of commandos north of Ossero which, after attacking the watchtower by capturing two legionnaires, blew up the bridge that connects Cres to Lošinj and the local barracks, after a few hours they re-embarked. The attacks were repeated on September 27th, with the participation of about 200 partisans, who attacked Ossero again, but were signaled by a strong reaction by the garrison that rejected the attackers, on November 17 and December 3. The latter operation was supported by the destroyers "Lauderdale" and "Eggsford" who, keeping the defenses of the island busy with a barrage, allowed the landing of the commandos in Porto Colorat. The action aimed to destroy the German base of the "Linse" boats, the Monte Asino battery of the Republican National Navy and the Mali Lošinj power plant, but the action did not achieve the expected results due to the strong reaction of the defenders. On the night between 8th and 9th March 1945 the S.B.S. he attempted a new attack on the barracks of Villa Punto, where there was a garrison of 16 soldiers with an officer. The attack, which lasted from 2 to 4.30, ended with the destruction of the barracks.

The commander of the Sauro Regiment was replaced on 13th February 1945 by Lieutenant Colonel Ruggero Melon, due to the difficult relationships that had been created with the Germanic authorities: Sauro was a staunch defender of the Italianness of Istria and this attitude was frowned upon by Germans. Libero Sauro was accompanied on his transfer from Pula to Koper by the "Iron Club"; before leaving, he carried out a final act of defiance to the anti-Italian anger of the German Commissioner Rainer, personally raising on a long flagpole an enormous tricolor flag, in front of the command of the "Istria" Regiment, also delivering a fervent speech imbued with Italian spirit[9].

---

[9] The German Command had in fact imposed on the Command of the 2nd Regiment in Pula to lower the tricolor flag, citing, as an explanation, that the presence of Italian symbols impacted the susceptibility of the members of the Slavic Polesan Party.

The Command of the 2nd "Istria" Regiment with the remains of the 1st Battalion, militarily framed, broke up in Koper on the morning of April 30th, 1945. The unit, while it was folding neatly over Trieste, was reached by the order of dissolution, in following the failed agreement with the CLN of Trieste and Istria, an agreement that had to find an agreement to defend the city in a united way from the arrival of the IX Korpus of Titus. Against the will of the military commander of the C.L.N. Colonel Peranna, the majority of the National Liberation Committee (which did not include the partisans of communist extraction) opted for a defense that excluded the soldiers of the R.S.I., not even under the command of the Italian partisans. Soldiers from the Civic Guard, some marines from the "San Giusto" Battalion of the Tenth and individual volunteers from other Republican departments joined the agreement. Some of these men ended up victims of the cannon fire of the German motorboats that were retreating to the Gulf of Trieste. The city was thus effectively handed over to the Titian occupier, with the belief that he would come to free it from the Nazi yoke. A partial exculpation of these lies the fact, unique in the history of the "liberation", that not a single shot was fired against the brothers: while in the rest of Italy the "hunt for the fascist" went mad, in Trieste a drop of blood.

At the end of the 2nd Battalion the news is practically null, it is known that the folding towards Koper began after having gathered the Departments in Vodnjan, but, in an unknown location, the column was stopped by the partisans who managed to bring together the officers with a stratagem and to arrest them, having so easy success on the soldiers left without command.

Part of the III Battalion surrendered on 1st May in Pieris sull'Isonzo, while a group remained in arms until 22th June, thanks also to the collaboration of the Italian peasants, ending the war almost 60 days after the official end of the conflict. The 2nd "Istria" Regiment was thus the last weapons department of the R.S.I. to lower their flag.

Organization chart

- Headquarter (Pula, then Villa Mosconi in Portorož)

    - Commander: Lieutenant Colonel Libero Sauro, replaced, in November 1944, by Colonel Ruggero Melon upon imposition of the German Command.

    - Major Assistant: Captain Bruno Sambo, then Major Antonino Alfano

    - Supplies: Captain Carlo Bacchetta

    - Administration: Major Elio Eliogabalo

    - U.P.I .: Maggiore Moscati, later Lieutenant Mastrogiovanni

- Women's Auxiliary Service Unit, consisting of 12 Auxiliaries[10]

---

[10] S.A.F. Unit Commander was Clara Del Fabbro from Trieste; the Auxiliary Licia Bilucaglia, daughter of the Federal of Pula was present at the regimental barracks in Medulin. Both had participated, in 1942, in the war film "Alfa Tau".

- Officers and Non-comissioned Officers School (Pula)
    - Commander: Major Ruggiero Melon, later Major Antonino Alfano
- School for soldiers C.A.M. (Pieris and S. Stefano d'Istria), was dissolved in mid 1944
    - Commander: Major Luigi Mosconi
- Verbindungsoffizier: Hauptmann Muller
- 1st Battalion (Capodistria later Buie) - Captain Possa subsequently Major Armando Martini
    - 1st Company "Trillo del Diavolo" (Koper with detachments in Piran, Isola, Corte d'Isola, Sicciole) - Commander: Captain Bonifacio
    - 2nd Company "Garibaldina" (Buje with detachments in Brtonigla, Castelvenere, Villa Gardossi, Umag, Grožnjan, Villanova del Quieto) - Commander: Captain Antonio Possa
    - 3rd Company "Unghia di Leone" (Motovun with detachments in Levade, Portole, Santo Stafeno, Caroiba, Visinada, Villa Treviso, Ponte Porton, Castellier di Visinada) - Commander: Captain Facchini, later Lieutenant Klausberger, Lieutenant Papo, Lieutenant Gera
    - Company "Adriatica" (Porec with detachments in Vrsar and Visignano)
- 2nd Battalion (Dignano) - Commander: Major Mignani subsequently Major Antonino Alfano
    - 4th Company "Dalmata" (Vodnjan with detachments in Roveria, Rovinj Valley, Rovinj, San Vincenti, Fažana, Brioni, Pazin)
    - 5th Company "Istriana" (Pola with detachments in Gallesano, Marzana, Giadreschi, Sichici, Sissano, Centrale Gas) - Commander: Lieutenant Vardabasso, subsequently Captain Bacchetta
    - 6th Company "Mazziniana" (Arsia with detachments at Santa Domenica d'Albona, Sumberesi, Barbana d'Istria, Pozzo Littorio, Valmazzinghi, mining complex of Arsia) - Commander: Captain Ottavio Rosolin
- 3rd Battalion (Aurisina until 16th April 1945 then Buzet Station), was established in January 1945 by transferring men from the other two Battalions, contracts to 3 Companies each - Commander: Captain Ottavio Rosolin, subsequently Captain Antonio Possa then Captain Tedeschi
    - 7th Company (Monfalcone with detachments in Sassetto and Acquaviva Valmorosa) - Commander: Lieutenant Domenico Italiano; Employees: Brigadieri Fiumi and Scindelli

- 8th Company (Aurisina, later Piedemonte del Tajano) - Commander: Lieutenant Bruno Manzin

- 9th Company (Castel Lupogliano) - Commander: Captain Bruno Artusi

- Autonomous Company "Tramontana" (Cres with detachments in Caisole, Ossero, Merganser, Dragosetti, Veli Lošinj, Punta Santa Croce) - Lieutenant Stefano De Petris[11].

- "Mazza di Ferro" Mobile Company (Pula) - Captain Bruno Artusi, later Lieutenant Fausto Vardabasso, then Lieutenant Klausberger (this Company was employed in the escort of the autocolumns).

The Regiment constituted a total of 43 detachments throughout Istria and another 7 in the provinces of Trieste and Gorizia, for the surveillance of the localities and the control of the territory.

In August 1944, the Germans wanted to impose a new line on the Regiment:

- Command and 1st Battalion in Pola, with detachments in Marzana, Barbana and Arsia

- 2nd Battalion in Dignano with detachments in Gallesano, Valle, Sanvincenti and Canale di Leme

- 3rd Battalion in Visinada with detachments in Montona, Caroiba, Pisino, Mompaderno and San Lorenzo

However, this deployment was not implemented due to the firm opposition of Lieutenant Colonel Sauro.

According to a report by the commander Sauro to Mussolini, at the end of November 1944 the 2nd "Istria" Regiment had a staff of about 1,000 men. In February 1945 the regiment consisted of 48 officers and 834 among non-commissioned officers and legionaries. To the soldiers in force in the Regiment, it is necessary to add the hundreds of civilians who, during the night and in case of emergencies, were armed and, wearing a tricolor band on their arm, replaced the legionaries in guarding the various positions. They were the so-called "Auxiliaries", generally old men who paid hundreds of lives for the defense of the Italianness of Istria.

Losses

Overall, the Regiment had 450 casualties, of which 210 after the end of the war. To this fallen number we must add all the "auxiliaries" who fell in combat alongside the legionaries of the Regiment.

---

11 Lieutenant Stefano De Petris, Chersino, animator of the resistance on the island of Cres, was captured by the Slavs, imprisoned in Rijeka and sentenced to death, a sentence that was carried out on 11th October 1945 near the Sussak cemetery.

▲ Flag of the 60th "Istria" Legion of the M.V.S.N., used after the Armistice by the homonymous 2nd Regiment of the Territorial Defense Militia (Crippa).

▼ The long-awaited moment of delivery of the mail to some legionaries of the M.D.T. in Istria in May 1944 (Arena).

▲ Bilingual signs such as this indicated the areas declared "Bandengebeit", that is infested by the partisan bands. In particular, in the photograph there is an indication of a dangerous area along the Cividale del Friuli – Udine road (Pisanò).

▲ Mortar gunners of a unit of M.D.T. while attacking partisan positions. The photograph was taken in the late spring of 1944, since the legionaries still have the M thunderbolts on the black flames on their lapels, which will be replaced by the sword only during the summer (Crippa).

▼ Autumn 1944: series of propaganda images depicting legionaries of the 2nd M.D.T. in action (Pisanò).

▲ Another image taken in the same mortar position: the soldier portrayed wears an M33 helmet with the old frieze of the M.V.S.N., a fairly common habit among legionnaires from the dissolved Milizia (Crippa).

▲ Propaganda image showing a legionnaire of the M.D.T. while stopping an alleged partisan, impersonated by one of his badly disguised comrades (Pisanò).

▲ A non-commissioned officer and an officer simulating an attack: the officer has an American-made gun, probably recovered from airborne material by the Allies, intended for the Slav partisans (Pisanò).

▼ The reconstruction of the attack on a cottage used by the partisans as a support base continues (Pisanò).

▲ Another image taken on the same occasion as the previous ones, which portrays militants of the M.D.T. intent on defending a railway line (Pisanò).

▼ The shot allows you to clearly identify, on the uniform of the legionary who throws a hand grenade, the badges, identical to those of the G.N.R., also adopted by the M.D.T. (Pisanò).

▲ Although it is a photo reconstruction for propaganda purposes, the defense of the railways, very important to ensure transports especially in Istria and for this reason often made signs of attacks by partisans, was one of the tasks to which the Regiments of the Militia (Pisanò).

▼ It is interesting to note the presence of the frieze of the dissolved M.V.S.N. on the M33 helmet of the legionary in the foreground (Pisano).

"Mazza di Ferro" Company

Let's briefly explore the history of the "Iron Mace" Company, which represented a unicum within the M.D.T., as the only armored department. The Company was based in Pula and was initially commanded by Captain Bruno Artusi, former lieutenant of the Bersaglieri; it was considered the mobile department of the Regiment, given the great availability of means of transport and armored vehicles. In fact, the Company was able to dispose of numerous vehicles, 2 L3 light tanks and some self-protected ones, built on truck chassis. Captain Artusi was later replaced by Lieutenant Fausto Vardabasso, who, in turn, passed the command of the Company to Lieutenant Egidio Klausberg. The tasks of the "Mazza di Ferro" were the escort to the autocolumns, the emergency service and the connection between the republican principals of Istria.

The light tanks of the ward were two armored vehicles abandoned by the Royal Army at the time of the Armistice. One of the two was purchased by an Istrian peasant, who had assembled a certain number of military vehicles abandoned in a sort of deposit, paying him 35,000 lire at the time; the cart was devoid of machine guns, which were soon recovered, however. The "Mazza di Ferro" instead came into possession of the second chariot, after it had been abandoned first by the Italian military and then by the Titian partisans, bartering it with… a truck loaded with shoes and clothing! It was mainly British material, captured by the legionaries during an airborne intended for partisans. One of the wagons, immobilized due to mechanical problems, was used as a basement in a strategic position at the entrance of the town of Buje and was destroyed by the same legionaries of the department on April 29th, 1945 with shots of hand grenades during the folding towards Koper. The other L3, which was used continuously in action and then also used as a fixed location in Koper, was thrown into the sea in the city port by the Rutter refueling officer, fearing that it could fall into the hands of the partisans by Tito.

The efficient regimental garage also transformed some trucks into self-protected ones, armored them with metal plates, side shields equipped with slits and protective nets against the throwing of hand grenades. These protected trucks, in charge of the "Mazza di Ferro" Company, were also armed with complexes of machine guns coupled by 13.2 mm from submarine, recovered at the large Arsenal of the Navy in Pola, or with a 20/65 machine gunner. These self-protected vehicles had disparate origins, in part, as we have seen, they were means obtained by field modification, in others of vehicles of the Royal Army, which were fortunately recovered and restored to efficiency. It can be seen in a photograph, for example, how two FIAT 665NM Scudato trucks of the Company were equipped with a turret made with a simple sheet metal cylinder, placed to defend the body of the body. It is difficult to establish precisely how many self-protected items were made for the "Iron Mace", although some sources set the number of vehicles of this type used by the Company at 6. From photographic and documentary sources it was possible to safely establish that a FIAT 626 was used in the department with the standard shields of the "older brother" FIAT 665 NM, evidently adapted to fit them on this truck, an armored Lancia 3 RO and at least two FIAT 665 NM Scudato.

The columns and garrisons of the Regiment were hit by continuous and repeated attacks, of ever-increasing violence, which in some cases, given the possibility of defending themselves, led to the complete annihilation of the contingents of the department. The mobile units, supported by armored vehicles, participated in mopping up operations, also in concert with the other units present in the region. In this perilous situation, the armored vehicles of the "Iron Mace" allowed to supply the garrisons scattered both along the coast and in the interior of Istria, escorting the truck that weekly carried out this vital task. The column was generally composed of one or two self-protected vehicles, trucks and a couple of motorcyclists, who preceded the vehicles to locate mines and explosive devices, which may have been placed on the roads by the partisans. Sometimes vehicles from other units and civilian vehicles also joined the regimental column, who took advantage of the escort of armored vehicles to travel more safely.

Some self-protected soldiers were posted to the regiment garrisons, to support the activity of the legionaries in the areas that were most dangerous, for example in Buje and Arsia. The self-protected ones were often made a sign of partisan attacks, with sometimes lethal consequences. The spring of 1944, in particular, was dotted with repeated ambushes on the armored vehicles of the "Iron Club". Recall for example that on 9th May the self-protected Arsia suffered a first partisan attack, on the road from Pula to Albona, which fortunately had no consequences. On the 27th of the same month the same self-protected ended in an escarpment following the outbreak of a mine and the heavy fire of automatic weapons, causing the death of a legionnaire and the wounding of 8 others.

On June 13th, 1944, the garrison of Arsia organized a truck to go to the rescue of the stronghold of Santa Domenica dAlbona, surrounded by preponderant partisan forces; the column was led by a self-protected from the same garrison of Albone. The next day another protégé, led by the legionary Emilio Bosiaco di Portale, was the victim of a mine explosion, while from the command of Pola he went to Arsia, to have news of the fighting taking place on Santa Domenica. After the bomb went off, the protected car was hit by a strong enemy fire and nine of the ten legionaries who made up the crew were tortured and killed; only one managed to escape and reach Marzana, although seriously injured. The corpses of the soldiers were brought to Pula for the solemn military funeral, decreed by the Regiment Command.

Dignano's self-protection was reported on July 28, when his crew came to the rescue of German soldiers engaged against the Slav partisans. The self-protected ones suffered numerous attacks even between the months of September and November of the same year. Recall that on October 21st the armored vehicles of the "Iron Mace" brought help to an Italian-German truck, putting the attackers to flight. On day 27th a protege of the 2nd Battalion of Dignano was unnecessarily targeted by the partisans, while escorting a German column near the crossroads of San Pietro in Selva - Pazin.

Interestingly, the commander of German Polizei himself in the O.Z.A.K. very often he required the escort of the "Mazza di Ferro" vehicles for the journeys he made by car in Istria.

On the evening of April 29th, 1945, after leaving Pula, the "Iron Club" reached Koper, where all the garrisons of the 1st Battalion and the Command of the "Istria" Regiment were gathering.

Here the commander of the Mobile Company, Lieutenant Egidio Klausberg, was informed that two of his soldiers, wounded the day before, had been left at the small hospital in Visinada. In the middle of the night the lieutenant, with a handful of men on board a small self-protected vehicle, reached Buje where, almost ignored by the partisans who already occupied the town, he recovered the two wounded, bringing them to safety in Koper. The following day the units of the Regiment, which hoped to reach Trieste to defend it from the Titian impetus, were reached by the dissolution order, which followed the failed agreement between the Republican forces and the C.L.N. Trieste, a fatal event that actually handed over the Friulian capital to the Slavs. However, a group of legionaries, including Lieutenant Klausberg, decided to continue to Trieste, where the small column melted, given the evolution of the situation. A self-protected chassis of a Lancia 3RO truck, which was part of the column, was voluntarily destroyed by the driver, who, after having dropped the occupants of the vehicle, launched the armored vehicle along a descent against a house, jumping outside. last moment. Sad was the end of the commander of the "Iron Mace" Klausberg: he was captured and killed on the outskirts of Koper on May 2nd, while returning from Trieste to his home in Piran.

▲ Legionary of a Regiment of the M.D.T. observe the movements of the patrols of the Slav partisans (Pisanò).

▲ Group of young students and instructor officers of the School of Pieris d'Isonzo (GO): this is the platoon commanded by Vice Brigadier Zago of the 1st M.D.T. Regiment (Roberti).

▼ A group of legionaries from the Territorial Defense Militia during a parade in the winter of 1944 - 1945 (Arena).

▲ Military School of Pieris, August 1944: the soldiers of the guardhouse (Roberti)

▼ Students and non-commissioned officers of the 2nd M.D.T. at the Military Training Center in September 1944 (Pisanò).

▲ Headquarters of the 3rd Company of the 2nd M.D.T. in Motovun (Papo).

▼ Fire Center Number 4 of the 3rd Company of the 2nd Regiment near the town of Motovun (Papo).

▲ Evocative image in which a legionary of the 2nd M.D.T. Behind the guard with the Reich flag and the tricolor of the R.S.I. (De Ferra).

▼ Bunker set up to defend a railway line manned by a group of men from the 2nd "Istria" Regiment (De Ferra).

3rd Regiment M.D.T. (61st Legion) "Carnaro"

At the end of December '43, the 61st Legion CC.NN. "Carnaro" had only the Territorial Battalion, for a total of 30 officers, 61 non-commissioned officers and 414 legionaries, including 216 young volunteers. With the influx of fascists, disbanded soldiers, sailors, financiers and carabinieri, in March 1944 the Legion was transformed into the 3rd M.D.T. "Carnaro", on two Battalions. The area belonging to the Regiment, although not very territorially extended, was very difficult due to the opposing interests that converged on the city of Rijeka. The activity was mainly aimed at controlling the territory and protecting the places inhabited by the Italians and to contain the dangers deriving from the strong presence in the area of Ustascia of Croats and Serbian Chetniks, animated by clear anti-Italian sentiments. The information aspect took on therefore the prevalence over the control of the territory and protection of localities inhabited by Italians. The 3rd Regiment did not have to undergo massive attacks, but continuous attacks and ambushes by G.A.P./V.O.S. who wore out the legionaries engaged in the hard patrol and escort service. Strong points were located Zaluche, Lippa, Mattuglie, Apriana, Laurana, Scalnizza, Ruppa, Velelasi. In the area of Rijeka, two Autonomous Companies M.D.T. Bordering, with garrisons between Giordani, Pusi, Sappiane, with frequent patrols for military recovery and territorial control. The activity of the U.P.I. he addressed himself in a particular way in defeating the clandestine slave organizations and of the Italian Communist Party, with a clear pro-Slavic tendency. There were numerous actions carried out by the soldiers who led to the capture of dozens of subversive elements that had bloodied with attacks, robberies, killers, forced withdrawals of men, the areas of Clana, Lippa, Scalnizza, Ruppa, Mune, Laurana. The most important result achieved by the U.P.I. of the 3rd "Carnaro" Regiment, it was the dismantling of the Slavic communist organization of Rijeka that took place in the summer of 1944, with the capture of dozens of people. In May 1944, units of the "Carnaro" Regiment participated in the security operations during the recovery of people thrown into the sinkholes in the Monte Maggiore area.

Many clashes occurred in the Sussak area, with a strong Croatian presence, with dozens of bomb attacks and damage to infrastructure and vehicles. Intense anti-guerrilla activity was carried out by the Departments lined up between Giordani, Pusi, Rupa di Elsane, Sappiane, with patrols, territorial controls, recovery of military material. The 3rd "Carnaro" Regiment ceased to exist between April 28th and 2th9 in Trieste. Two companies followed the retreating German troops and surrendered to Opatija, a hundred soldiers managed to reach Trieste.

Organization chart 3° Reggimento M.D.T. "Carnaro"

- Command (Fiume)

    - Commander: Lieutenant Colonel Giuseppe Porcu[12], replaced by Lieutenant Colonel Pietro Montesi Righetti.

---

[12] Lieutenant Colonel Porcu was exonerated, by the command of the Regiment, in February 1945 due to strong conflicts with the German authorities; returned to Trieste, he was arrested in the city on 5 May by OZNA agents. On the 20th he was taken from the Coroneo prison and taken to an unknown location, most likely in Yugoslavia. It is unknown where and when he was killed

- Major Assistant: Major Luigi Capellini subsequently Captain Nordico, Captain Angelo Meda, Captain Spaizzi.

- Administration Officer: Maggiore Carletti

- Officer at the freshman

- Service Officer

- Chaplain Officer: Lieutenant Alessandro Don Mandrini

- Speaker Officer

- Health Service Manager

- Verbindungsoffizier: Hauptmann Goll

- U.P.I.

- Regimental Command Company - Commander: Captain Franco De Franchi

- I Battalion (Fiume) - Commander: Major Arnaldo Viola subsequently Captain Carlo Carletti, Captain Angelo Meda, Captain Pietro Barbali

    - 1st Company – Commander: Captain Nordco, then Captain Meda, finally Lieutenant Barbali

    - 2nd Company – Commander: Lieutenant Battistini

    - 3rd Company – Commander: Captain La Gattola

- II Battalion (Abbazia) - Comandante: Major Armando Viola

    - 4th Company – Commander: Captain Bulian, later Captain De Franchi

    - 5th Company – Commander: Captain Bonanno

    - 6th Company – Commander: Captain Antonini

The staff of the 3rd "Carnaro" Regiment amounted to about 1,500 units in total, a number reached thanks to the influx of ex-Royal Army disbanded soldiers, sailors, fascists, Finance guards, G.a.F. and Carabinieri.

Losses

At the end of 1944, 47 legionnaires had fallen, and 21 others were missing, 38 injured. At the end of April 1945, the fallen numbered 258 men; the number of missing and missing people after the end of hostilities is not known.

▲ Portrait of a second lieutenant of the 2nd "Istria" Regiment, which allows to clearly identify the frieze of the cap, used by the departments of the M.D.T., with the number of the Regiment in the rod (Arena).

▲ Two young officers of the 2nd M.D.T. next to an 81 mm mortar in a garrison in Istria (De Ferra).

▼ Group of legionaries of the "Lion's Nail" Company of the 2nd Battalion of the "Istria" Regiment in Motovun (Arena).

▲ The young Lieutenant Nino Arena, who will become famous after the war for his extensive publications concerning the units of the Italian Social Republic, photographed on license in Venice, while serving as a newly appointed officer at the 2nd Territorial Defense Militia Regiment (Arena).

▲ On the left of the photo, Lieutenant De Petris, commander of the "Tramontana" Company with some soldiers from the garrison of the island of Cres (Arena).

▲ Major Antonino Alfano, Major Adjutant of the "Istria" Regiment, visits the garrisons of the island of Cres, accompanied by Lieutenant Stefano De Petris and a legionary. The mule was a convenient form of transportation on the treacherous roads of the island. (Arena).

▼ A photograph, unfortunately of poor quality, which portrays a group of soldiers from the "Tramontana" Company on island of Cres having lunch with some civilians (Arena).

▲ Even the most ordinary activities, such as cooking, were carried out by the chefs of the "Tramontana" Company with the utmost dedication (Arena).

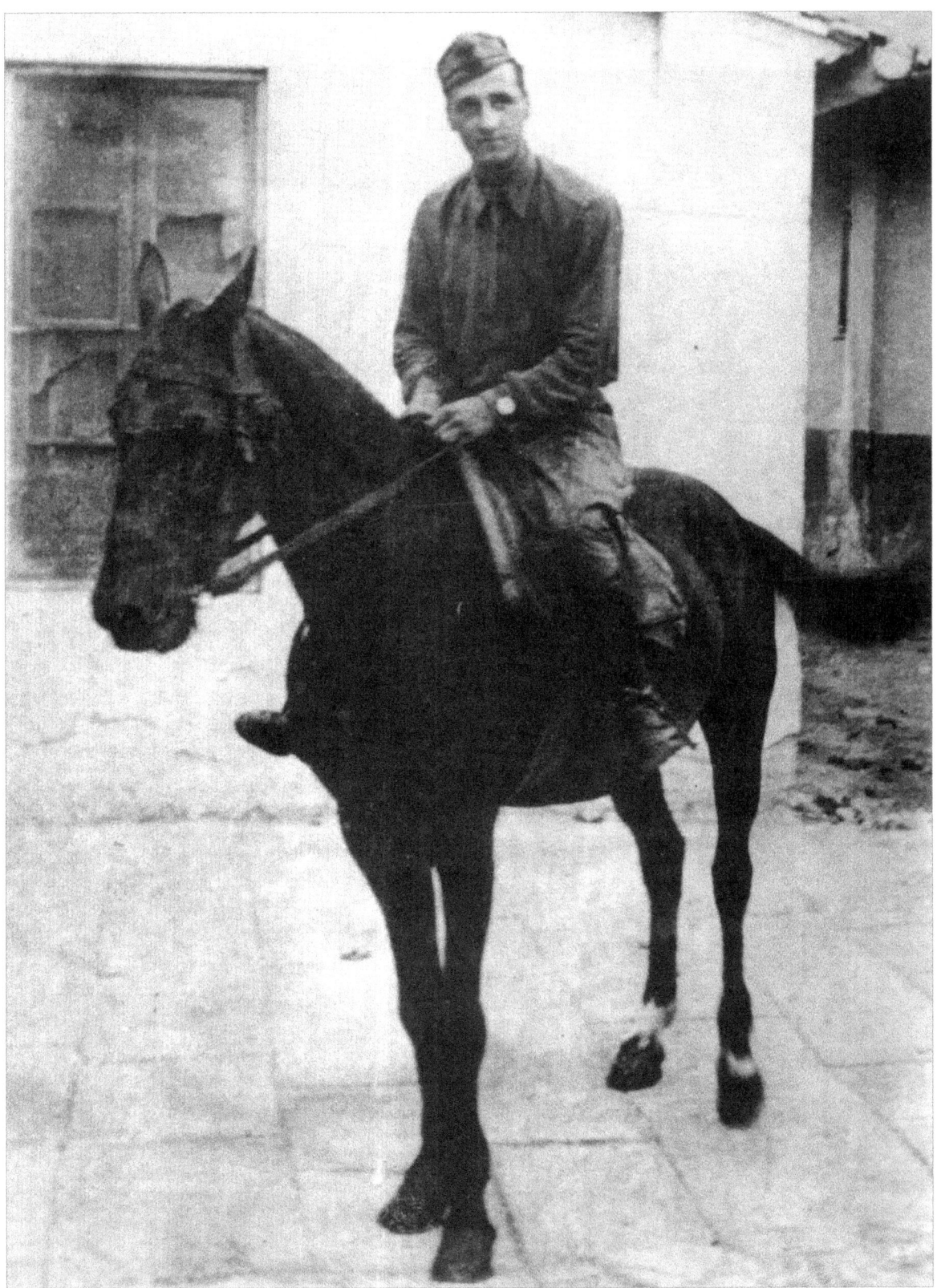

▲ Lieutenant Mariano Apollonio of the "Istria" Regiment, who was killed by a barrage of machine guns on April 13th, 1944 after having staunchly defended the garrison of Santa Domenica d'Albona with his subordinates (Arena).

▲ The soldier Roberti, the Lieutenant Samsa and the soldier Ferretti of the 2nd "Istria" Regiment at the Monrupino station in winter 1944 (Roberti).

▲ Group of soldiers of the 1st Battalion of the 2nd M.D.T. in Valle Fricola in January 1945 (Papo).

▼ Group of officers of the 1st Battalion of the 2nd M.D.T. at the cathedral of Buje on March 19th, 1945. Between the two senior officers, in the center, we note the German police captain who acted as liaison officer (De Ferra).

▲ On 1st May 1945 in San Giovanni al Timavo (TS) the flag of the III Platoon of the 7th Company of the 3rd Battalion of the 2nd Territorial Defense Militia Regiment, last unit of the R.S.I. that surrendered (Arena).

▲ Graphic elaboration of the emblem of the 2nd Arditi Company of the 3rd "Carnaro" Regiment of the M.D.T. (Quattrocchi).

▼ Soldiers of the 3rd Regiment of the Territorial Defense Militia during a moment of leisure. The turret behind it was used for anti-aircraft sighting (Pisanò).

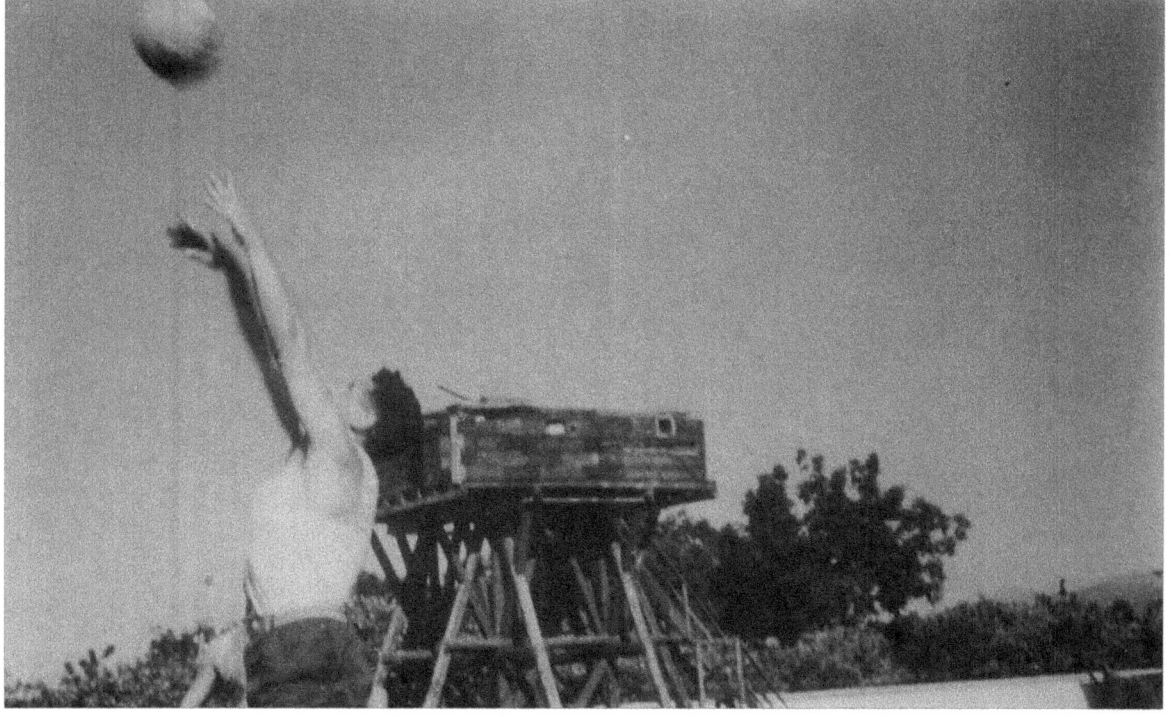

▲ Civil and military authorities present at a demonstration in Gorizia during 1944. From the left in plain clothes the Prefect Marino, next to him with the alpine hat the Federal og Republican Fascist Party Frattarelli (proud opponent of the German interference in Venezia Giulia), the Lieutenant Colonel Rocco, commander of the 4th MDT Regiment, Lieutenant Colonel La Mendola, who will succeed Rocco in command of the Regiment, Colonel Greco and Colonel Ruggero of the Regional Military Command (Arena).

▼ A jubilant group of legionaries of the 4th M.D.T. aboard a truck in the Gorizia area. Some of them continue to wear the black fez of the dissolved M.V.S.N. (Arena).

4th Regiment M.D.T. (62nd Legion) "Gorizia"

The 4th "Gorizia" Regiment originated from the 62nd Legion CC.NN. which, in October 1943, had about 400 soldiers, including 24 officers, 48 non-commissioned officers, 230 legionnaires and 98 volunteers, under the command of the Consul Urbano Rocco. Between November of that year and the month of March of the following year, another 800 volunteers joined the soldiers already in service, thus allowing the creation of two Battalions. These volunteers came largely from the dissolution of the 4th Legion G.N.R. of Frontier and they went to establish an Autonomous Border Battalion M.D.T. for mobile use, an Autonomous Company in Tolmezzo and the two Autonomous Companies of Rijeka, part of which were then transferred to the Gorizia and included in the 4th Regiment. When, in the summer of 1944, the Germans ordered the dissolution of the Carabinieri, a large group of 400 military men from them passed through the 4th M.D.T. "Gorizia", being placed in the 2nd Battalion. From the bases of the Battalions located in Gorizia and Cormons, garrisons were set up in the main towns of the province: Savogna d'Isonzo, Lucinico, Piedimonte del Calvario, San Lorenzo Isontino, Aidussina, Aisovizza, Fontefredda, Rupa, San Pietro di Gorizia, Mossa, Sant'Andrea, Monte Santo, Farra d'Isonzo, Medea, Gradisca, Sagrado, Moncorona, Salcano, Plava, Piuma, Piuma bridge, Ronchi dei Legionari. The Carabinieri were divided between Gorizia and Gradisca. The activity of the units of the 4th M.D.T. Regiment "Gorizia" took place by arranging surveillance and protection services for strategic plants such as railways, bridges, viaducts, power and water plants, tunnels and industrial plants. The small number of staffs, combined with the vastness of the area of competence, forced the Superior Command of the M.D.T. to send other Regiments of the M.D.T. and unit of the E.N.R. in support of the action of the 4th "Gorizia". The units were thus engaged in territorial control, carried out in collaboration with these other departments of the R.S.I., in the province and in the valleys of Baccia, Vipacco and Alto Isonzo. An Anti-Aircraft Platoon of the Regiment, armed with 3 German 20mm machine guns, in position at the old sports field, defended the road and railway bridges over the Isonzo in Gorizia. Very important is the activity of the U.P.I. (political office), aimed at the dismantling of the slave and Italian communist clandestine formations, as well as the control of the anti-Italian activities of the various collaborative formations of Domobrani, Cetnic and Belagardists, of clear anti-communist sentiments, but also anti-Italian and deeply nationalist. The U.P.I. he managed to identify informants and supporters of the Yugoslav Communist Party in Verpogliano and Vipacco, dismantling an organization dedicated to the collection of food for the local Karaule. Other important successes were achieved in Merna, in March 1944, in May, in the lower Karst area between Ranziano, Biglia, Prevacina, Merna, Vertoiba, San Pietro di Gorizia, with the discovery of the command of the local Karaula responsible for dozens of attacks, sabotages, killings, in July in the Valvociana area and in August in the Collio area. Precisely in consideration of the important successes collected against the Titian partisans and the Italian communists, in the spring of 1945, at the head of the U.P.I. Lieutenant Colonel Paolo Nitti and later Major Giovanni Gonano were assigned. The attacks of the partisans, to the garrisons and detachments scattered throughout the territory, had already started in the last months of 1943: on November 17th in Plava, in early December in Piedimonte del Calvario, on the 18th at the railway station of Gorizia, in the following days a power plant was destroyed and a train was derailed between San Pietro del Carso and Divaccia, on 29th December the barracks of S.

Lorenzo in Mossa were attacked and the next day that of Aisovizza. But it was in 1944 that the attacks intensified considerably, with continuous attacks on the garrisons of the Regiment, on the inhabited centers where Italians resided (for example, remember the attack on the "Verdi" theater in Gorizia on August 5th, 1944) and on the railway lines (the worst of which on September 9th at the Rubbia / San Michele - Gradisca / San Martino railway). The activity of the 4th M.D.T. Regiment was therefore intense and multifaceted, both on a purely defensive and informative level, essential in the complex and difficult situation of the Gorizia area. The most tragic event, which involved the 4th M.D.T. "Gorizia", took place on April 16th, 1945 at the checkpoint in San Pietro di Gorizia, when the local garrison, which was to receive the change from a department of Cetnici, while it was lined up for the small flag, at a signal from a German non-commissioned officer, was exterminated by the Serbs. The regiment ceased to exist between April 29th and 30th in Gorizia.

Organization chart 4th Regiment M.D.T. "Gorizia"

- Headquarter (Gorizia)
    - Commander: Consul Urbano Rocco, later Lieutenant Colonel Vincenzo La Mendola, then Colonel Antonio Zambelli
    - Major Assistant: Captain Moro
- U.P.I. - Commander: Colonnell Rocco later Lieutenant Colonel Nitti then Major Gonano
- Verbindungsoffizier: Hauptmann Paul
- 1st Battalion (Gorizia) - Commander: Major Mario De Ferri later Captain Orlando De Lena, then Major Efisio Defenu, finally Major Giuseppe Caloro
    - 1st Company: Captain Dilena
    - 2nd Company
- 2nd Battalion (Cormons) - Commander: Captain Giuseppe Vecchiati, later Major Giuseppe Caloro, finally Major Angelo Meda.
    - 3rd Company: Lieutenant Toricelli
    - 4th Machine-gun Company

To these units it is necessary to add the Border Battalion and the Autonomous Border Companies. The maximum staff reached by the "Gorizia" Regiment was about a thousand men, in February 1945 the 4th Regiment had a staff of 28 officers and 665 among non-commissioned officers and soldiers.

Losses

At the end of October 1944 there were 104 confirmed casualties, 118 wounded, 199 missing to be considered fallen. According to the various sources consulted, the overall casualties of the "Gorizia" regiment vary from 119 to 170.

▲ Platoon of soldiers of the 4th "Gorizia" Regiment in charge of the defense of the bridges over the Isonzo (Francesconi).

▼ Young legionaries of the 4th M.D.T. during a ceremony in front of the castle of Gorizia (Arena).

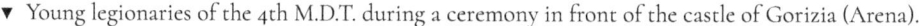

▲ Soldier of the 4th "Gorizia" Regiment mounts the guard at the entrance to the headquarters of the 3rd "Santa Gorizia" Company in September 1944 (Pisanò).

▼ Alessandro Pavolini, Secretary of the Republican Fascist Party, visited the Adriatic coast in January 1945, at a particularly difficult time for the Julian population. In this image, Pavolini receives the honors from a picket of militiamen of the "Gorizia" Regiment, while he enters the Provincial Command of the Territorial Defense Militia of Gorizia (Arena).

▲ The remains of the monument to the fallen of the Great War of Gorizia, designed by Enrico Del Debbio between 1925 and 1929. A bomb attack was made on the night of August 12th, 1944 as a sign of contempt by "white" Slavs, with the Germans' approval (Arena).

▼ Pavolini in Gorizia, gathered in meditation at the ruins of the monument, to which some soldiers of the 4th Militia Regiment mount their guard. Pavolini's visit was strongly opposed by the German authorities. (Arena).

5th Regiment M.D.T. (63rd Legion) "Friuli"

The 5th "Friuli" Regiment originated from the 63rd Legion CC.NN. "Val Tagliamento" whose commander, Primo Seniore Attilio De Lorenzi, on the date of September 8th, occupied and defended, with his legionaries, warehouses and military depots until the arrival of the German troops, and from the 55th Legion CC.NN. "Alpina Friulana". At the end of 1943 the unit had reached a staff of about 750 men, including young volunteers and legionary elders already in service, with 40 officers and 155 non-commissioned officers. In early April 1944, the 63rd Legion CC.NN. was transformed into the 5th M.D.T. "Friuli". With the continuous influx of volunteers, it was possible to set up 5 Battalions plus a Complement Battalion, resulting in the M.D.T. more numerous. In addition to carrying out the duties of supervision and institute in the area of competence, the 5th M.D.T. "Friuli" was engaged in mopping up operations in Carnia, in the defense of garrisons in the Val Vipacco, on the Trieste Karst and in the Postumia sector, an activity carried out against the partisans of the Slavic IX Korpus. The operational area entrusted to the 5th "Friuli" Regiment was infested with numerous fierce and well-armed partisan formations, both Italian such as the communist "Garibaldi" and the monarchic "Osoppo", and Slavic, belonging to the IX Korpus. The clashes with the partisans followed a continuous growing month after month, with dozens of attacks on the garrisons and detachments scattered throughout the territory. On April 25th, 1944 the garrison of Tolmezzo was attacked, while in May the one of Paluzza and between 26th and 28th there was a series of clashes in Tabor, Sassetto, Rifembergo. In June the garrisons of Vergnacco, Poianis, Sassetto, Saga, Ponte San Quirino were targeted, while in July there were clashes Verzegnis, Gemona, Cividale, at the powder keg of Santa Margherita, in Rifembergo, at the roadblock on the Tolmezzo road- Paluzza, in San Pietro al Natisone and at the Trivio di Colidin and, throughout the summer, the Regiment was engaged in constant clashes throughout the area of operations. From 2nd to 10th October, two Companies of the Regiment attacked the partisan positions in the area of the Braulins bridge, Trasaghis, Avasinis and Alesso, while from 8th to 23th an extensive operation was carried out against the Free Zone of Friuli. Even the winter was characterized by constant fighting against the partisans and in all these dozens of attacks, suffered or carried out, the departments of the 5th "Friuli" Regiment suffered dozens of Fallen, missing and injured. The activity of the U.P.I. of the 5th M.D.T. "Friuli" made it possible to identify numerous communist elements, who kept the links with the partisan bands, discovering a pro-Slavic autonomist current and proceeding to arrest the members, also exposing some Italian police officers who were in connection with the partisans.

▲ After the explosion, the monument was kept in ruins in perpetual memory of what happened. For a time, a courageous sign headed the pile of rubble: "The Italian spirit of Gorizia is not destroyed by hitting the monuments to the fallen for the freedom of Italy!" (Arena).

Organization chart 5th Regiment M.D.T. "Friuli"

- Command (Udine)
  - Commander: Colonel Attilio De Lorenzi
  - 1st Assistant Major: Major Attilio Barbacetto
  - Major Adjutant in 2nd: Captain Bruno Castelletti
  - Administration Officer
  - Mobilization and Registration Officer
  - Transportation Materials Officer
  - Health Service Manager
  - Chaplain Officer: Lieutenant Aristide Don Baldassi
  - Official "I": Major Evaristo Caroi
  - U.P.I.
  - Verbindungsoffizier: Hauptmann Hasenfuss, later Hauptmann Schultze
- Deposit Company - Commander: Captain Arturo Vittorino
- Road M.D.T. unit - Commander: Assistant Luigi Izzo

Commander for columns: Brigadier Renato Quadraroli

- I Battalion – Commander: Major Italo Tomassetti later Captain Italo Apollonio
  - 1st Company - Commander: Captain Matteotti, Captain Venier
  - 2nd Company - Commander: Captain Capitano Vetturini, Captain Ruggero
  - 3rd Company - Commander: Captain Collovini, Captain Facchin

It was based in Manzano and Muzzana and had offices in Comeno, Rifembergo-Castello, Saletto, Rifembergo-Stazione, Trieste, Scoppo, Duttogliano, Crepegliano, Monrupino, Muzzana del Turgnano, San Giorgio di Nogaro, Pordenone.

- II Battaglione - Commander: Major Francesco Del Giudice
  - 4th Company - Commander: Captain Gonano
  - 5th Company
  - 6th Company

It was based in Tarvisio and Gemona and was deployed with garrisons to protect the Udine - Tarvisio railway line and military installations in the area itself and in the Gorizia area.

- III Battalion - Commander: Captain Giannino Giannini, subsequently Major Gaspare Aita
  - 7th Company
  - 8th Company
  - 9th Company

Based in San Leonardo and Plezzo, it had garrisons in the Natisone and Isonzo Valleys, from Cividale to Plezzo, and in Valcellina from Montereale to Erto and Casso. The 9th Company also carried out institutional duties at the prisons of Udine.

- IV Battalion (Friulian Fascists Battalion) - Commander: Captain Gino Covre subsequently Captain Walter Bruno Pozzi[13]
  - 1st later 10th Company – Commander: Captain Capitano Cesare Bastianutti
  - 2nd later 11th Company - Commander: Captain Francesco Venier
  - 3rd later 12th Company

Located in Artegna and Pontebba, it was used as a mobile department, starting from Udine.

- V Special Services Battalion (formed by the Carabinieri after the dissolution of the unit

---

[13] According to other sources, the second Commander of the IV Battalion was Major Ernesto Morassutti.

imposed by the Germans) - Commander: Lieutenant Colonel Agostino Vittucci subsequently Lieutenant Colonel Pietro Ramolfo1ª later 13ª Company
- 1st later 13th Company
- 2nd later 14th Company
- 3rd later 15th Company

It was deployed to Udine and its province.
• Complements Battalion (Udine) - Commander: Lieutenant Colonel Ugo Macuglia
- 1st later 16th Company
- 2nd later 17th Company
- 3rd later 18th Company
- 4th later 19th Special Company (composed of former enlisted partisans)

It carried out training and protection of public interest plants.

An autonomous Company of Border M.D.T. was detached in Tolmezzo under the command of Captain Hosmer Zimbelli, while a Boundary Company was detached in Tarvisio under the command of Captain Vittorio Falcone. On October 31st, 1944 the strength of the 5th "Friuli" Regiment was as follows:
• Regimental Command: 12 officers, 36 non-commissioned officers and 33 soldiers, for a total of 81 men
• The Battalion: 14 officers, 31 non-commissioned officers and 208 soldiers, for a total of 251 men
• 2nd Battalion: 9 officers, 43 non-commissioned officers and 240 soldiers, for a total of 292 men
• 3rd Battalion: 10 officers, 9 non-commissioned officers and 188 soldiers, for a total of 207 men
• 4th Battalion: 19 officers, 58 non-commissioned officers and 184 soldiers, for a total of 261 men
• 5th Battalion: 7 officers, 105 non-commissioned officers and 334 soldiers, for a total of 446 men
• Complements Battalion: 10 officers, 79 non-commissioned officers and 264 soldiers, for a total of 353 men
• Deposito company: 7 officers, 56 non-commissioned officers and 627 soldiers, for a total of 690[14]
• Guardia di Finanza Autonomous Company: 4 officers, 34 non-commissioned officers and 243 soldiers, for a total of 281 men

Overall, therefore, on that date the Regiment consisted of 92 officers, 451 non-commissioned officers and 2319 soldiers, for a total of 2862 men[15]. According to the documentation found, in February 1945 the 5th Regiment had a staff of 85 officers and 1733 among non-commissioned officers and soldiers, probably without counting the staff of the Deposit Company.

Losses

At the end of October 1944 there were 194 confirmed dead, 118 injured and 199 missing to be considered fallen. The losses in the last months of the conflict can be estimated in about another hundred men, injured people excluded.

S.A.F. Preparation Center

For the staff of the Women's Auxiliary Service employed by the departments of the M.D.T. a special school was set up, the S.A.F. Preparation Center, located in Pula. The Center was in command of the Head of Unit Clara Del Fabbro.

M.D.T. Confinaria (Frontier)

M.D.T. Confinaria originated from M.V.S.N. di Frontiera, from which it inherited his duties: supervision of the passes, valleys, power plants and mountain roads. It was organized on 1 Battalion and 3 Autonomous Companies:

---
14 The data is extremely high and not justified
15 According to another source, the total staff of the 5th "Friuli" Regiment on the same date was 2,904 men.

- 1st Battalion M.D.T. Confinaria in Trieste[16] - Commander: Major Oderico Rieppi
- Autonomous Company M.D.T. Confinaria in Tolmezzo - Commander: Captain Hosner Zimbelli
- Autonomous Company M.D.T. Confinaria in Fiume - Commander: Lieutenant Antonio Facchetti
- Autonomous Company M.D.T. Confinaria in Tarvisio - Commander: Captain Vittorio Falcone

These new units were entrusted with direct surveillance of the areas immediately adjacent to the border line, with the task of ensuring that no pass, or glues, or access, however difficult, could escape control and allow infiltrations of titian partisans..

M.D.T. Speciali (Specials)

Just as happened for G.N.R., also M.D.T. inherited from the ranks of the dissolved M.V.S.N., the so-called Special Militias, those departments specifically set up to perform well-identified institution tasks: Postelegrafonica (Postal), Forestale (Forestry), Ferroviaria (Railway), Portuale (Port Authorithy) and Stradale (Road). The great majority of the Special Militia soldiers came from the ranks of the pre-existing units, although young soldiers were present, who had asked for enrollment in these departments both voluntarily.

The units of the M.D.T. Specials were located between Trieste, Gorizia, Fiume, Pola and Udine, however covering the whole territory of the O.Z.A.K. even with small local offices:

- Milizia Difesa Territoriale Postelegrafonica
  - Comman: Trieste - Commander: Lieutenant Federico Raciti
  - Unit "Fiume" - Commander: Lieutenant Ciro Paliotti
- Milizia Difesa Territoriale Forestale
  - Detachments: Udine, Gorizia, Pola, Fiume
- Milizia Difesa Territoriale Portuale
  - M.D.T. Portuale Battalion in Trieste - Commander: Major Giovanni Roman
  - Detachments: Pola - Fiume (Commander: Captain Pietro Danieli)
- Milizia Difesa Territoriale Ferroviaria
  - M.D.T. Ferroviaria Battalion - Commander: Colonel Minacapilli
  - Units in Trieste e Trieste-Sea
  - Major Detachments: Fiume, Gemona, Gorizia, Mattuglie, Pola, Pontebba, Tarvisio, Udine
  - Detachments: Piedicolle, Canale d'Isonzo, Gorizia Montesanto
- Milizia Difesa Territoriale Stradale
- Numerically the M.D.T. Specials lined up:
- Postelegrafonica   160 men
- Forestale   180 men
- Ferroviaria   170 men
- Portuaria   120 men
- Stradale   130 men

for a total of no more than 760 men.

---

[16] Sometimes also referred to as "Mobile Border Battalion of the Territorial Defense Militia".

Armaments and uniforms of the M.D.T.

The individual armament distributed to the legionaries of the M.D.T. was typical of the Italian infantry of the beginning of the Second World War: '91 rifles and muskets, Breda 30 submachine guns, Beretta 34 pistols, a few MABs, hand grenades and, after the first months, also machine guns and submachine guns captured at partisans and Allied aircrafts. The team's armament consisted basically of Breda 37 and Fiat 35 machine guns, both in 8 caliber, 45mm and 81mm Brixia mortars. There were also some Italian 20mm machine-guns, used both in anti-aircraft function and for the support fire, also the 4th "Gorizia" Regiment had at least 3 20mm quadrilateral machine-guns, of German origin, in service for the anti-aircraft defense of the bridges.

The type of vehicles in service at the departments of the MDT Regiments is not known, nor their number, however from the photographic evidence and the testimonies of the veterans, it can be said that the vehicles in service had to be in sufficient number to guarantee operational needs. The regiments of the M.D.T. did not have armored cars or tanks in service, with the exception, as we have seen, of the 2nd Regiment "Istria".

The supply of uniforms and equipment was, for the soldiers of the M.D.T., very difficult, especially because of the German interference, which supplied the regiments with the dropper. For this reason, the situation was very confused: to dress and equip the soldiers, all the recoverable items from the warehouses of the dissolved Royal Army was recovered and therefore the variety of estates was very wide, as evidenced by the photographs. The uniforms of the dissolved Milizia in gray-green cloth were widespread, which were integrated, when possible, with the most practical paratrooper uniforms, always combined with the black shirt. The use of khaki summer uniforms has been poorly documented, while some camouflage garments and accessories were distributed, albeit in a limited number.

The headgear common to all the legionaries was the envelope cap, with rigid visor, but the sachet without a visor was also widespread and, for young people from the G.N.R. Schools, the black beret. The soldiers of the M.D.T. Confinaria and Forestale continued to wear the alpine cap. The G.N.R.'s badge was worn on the headgear, embroidered on a gray-green or black background, representing a stylized bundle, with two "M" arranged laterally and a rod below, at the center of which should have been the number of your Regiment, a prescription not always fulfilled.

The M33 helmet was obviously in use, on which the stamping of the same frieze of the caps was expected, although many legionaries continued to have the previous symbol of the M.V.S.N., as can be seen from the photographic evidence.

Initially all members of the M.D.T. wore the two-pointed black flames of M.V.S.N. with the golden bands, which gradually gave way to black flames with the silver "M" arrows, replaced by the sword with laurel starting from August 28th, 1944.

The regulation of the G.N.R. for Special Militias provided specific cap friezes, similar to those already in use by M.V.S.N. and a thread of different color to the flames, although it was not always possible to adapt:
- Postelegrafonica e Ferroviaria: red
- Forestale and Confinaria: green
- Portuaria: crimson
- Stradale: light blue.

▲ Colonel Attilio De Lorenzi, commander of the 5th "Friuli" Territorial Defense Militia Regiment (Pisanò).

▲ Legionaries of the "Friuli" Regiment guarding a railway line in the summer of 1944. Photography allows you to appreciate the equipment and armament of the soldiers of the M.D.T., based essentially on individual weapons of the Royal Army. Both have the dagger that was distributed to the members of the M.V.S.N. (Pisano).

▲ Anti-aircraft station, positioned on a wooden tower, of the 5th M.D.T. (Pisano).

▲ Soldiers of the Border M.D.T. on patrol (Arena).

▼ The group of soldiers from the Confinaria reach Piano d'Arta, a town near Tolmezzo, with the unit's flag in their heads (Pisanò).

▲ Sequence of images of the oath ceremony of a group of soldiers of the Autonomous Company of Border M.D.T. of Tolmezzo: the soldiers on the march (Pisanò).

▲ Deployment of the soldiers of the Autonomous Company of Border M.D.T. at attention (Pisanò).

▼ The most significant moment of the oath ceremony: the kiss to the Tricolor flag (Pisanò).

▲ The photos allow you to appreciate the uniform of these soldiers, which refers to the Alpine tradition, as they are engaged in the control of national borders (Pisanò).

BADGES OF MILIZIA DIFESA TERRITORIALE

Cap badge and two-pointed black flames with bundles of the dissolved M.V.S.N., used throughout 1943 by members of the Territorial Defense Militia

Arm shield of the "Mazza di Ferro" Company of 2nd "Istria" Regiment

BADGES OF MILIZIA DIFESA TERRITORIALE

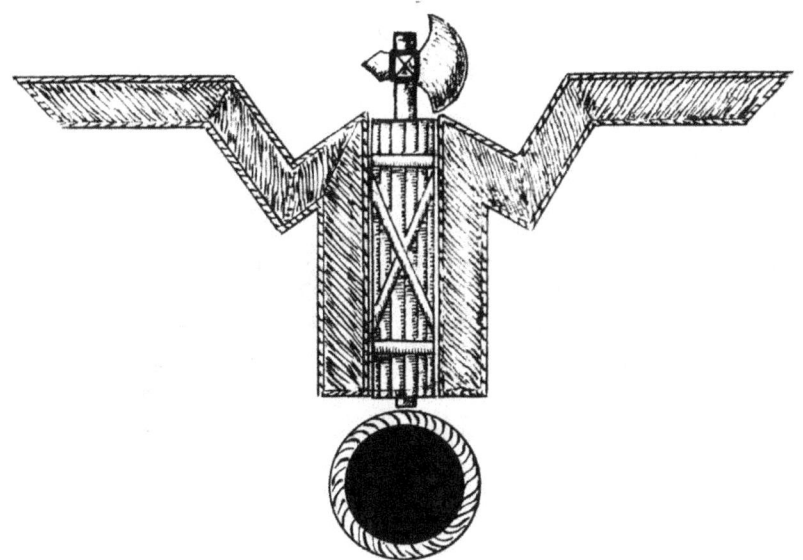

Cap badge adopted after the establishment of the G.N.R.

Black lapel's flames with lightning "M"

Black lapel's flames with gladios introduced since August 28th, 1944

CAP'S BADGES OF SPECIALS M.D.T.

M.D.T. Confinaria

M.D.T. Postelegrafonica

M.D.T. Forestale

M.D.T. Portuale

M.D.T. Ferroviaria

M.D.T. Stradale

CIVIC GUARDS IN THE O.Z.A.K.

After that the territories of Friuli and Istria were incorporated into the Reich, as a consequence of the Armistice of September 8th, the Carinthian Galautier Rainer, the highest German authority on O.Z.A.K., issued a notice in November 1943 which required the service of war on men skilled in arms, service to be provided to territorial defense forces or in the T.O.D.T. Organization. In fact, this ban placed young Italians in the face of the arduous choice of agreeing to serve in the German militias or of providing forced labor and the only possible alternatives to avoid this forced recruitment were or to present themselves as volunteers to the departments of the Social Republic[17], that were forming in the region, or to go into hiding, joining the Italian or Yugoslav partisan formations. The Germanic authorities soon realized that the majority of those recalled would have opted for these latter solutions and therefore had to run for cover, allowing the establishment of a paramilitary force with police duties, equipped with Italian uniforms and Italian officers, thanks also to the effort joint of the Prefect and the Podestà of Trieste[18]. Four military corps in Trieste, Gorizia, Capodistria and Pordenone were therefore established under the name "Civic Guard". The Civic Guards were perceived by German, Italian and population authorities in very different ways. In the first place, the Germans, in addition to having decreed the creation of the Civic Guards to avoid a hemorrhage of valid men towards other military forces or towards the partisan movements, conceived and organized these units with the aim of strengthening the containment structure of the movement partisan by inserting local elements, simultaneously leading to a progressive Germanization of the area. The Italian authorities, on the other hand, saw in the Civic Guards a good way to avoid forced enlistment in the workers' departments and in the German armed forces of vast layers of the population. Finally, for the inhabitants of the region, the enlistment in the Guards was seen, in a context of power absolutely in the balance, as a good compromise not to expose themselves excessively neither in support of the occupiers, nor of the Social Republic, nor of the resistance movement. This will ensure that the Civic Guards were in fact a congregation of anti-fascists, fascists and supporters of the Reich, exposing, especially in the last wartime periods, their own members of repressions coming from many parts.

Enrollment in the Civic Guard was advertised to the population as the possibility of becoming part of a locally based organization, employed in non-heavy and above all non-continuous tasks, which therefore allowed members to continue their daily lives on a regular basis, without leaving the family and losing their job[19]. In this regard, we quote the text of a poster that appeared at the end of 1943 in Isola (now Izola in Slovenia):

"The Civic Guard has the sole purpose of protecting public order in the city and safeguarding private property in the event of an emergency, excluding any other employment [...]. No continuous service is required so that every citizen can participate in this institution without prejudice to their interests and occupations"[20].

17 In reality, the Chief of General Staff Mischi reported that the percentage of volunteer members of the R.S.I. it was very low, enough to call it "depressing".
18 The idea was actually not completely new. In fact, for example, already in August 1942 the archbishop of Gorizia Monsignor Margotti sent a letter to the prefecture of the city, in which he supported the opportunity to create a militia on a local basis. The prelate suggested to *"[...] establish in each country a Civil Guard made up of local elements, capable, precisely for this reason, of being used effectively in the search and repression of the communist and partisan gangs"*.
19 The possibility of being able to continue to take care of their work and their affairs took hold above all on the bourgeoisie of the coastal areas, who adhered quite enthusiastically to the calls for enrollment for the Civic Guards, which represented for them a valid alternative to the resistance movement, loaded of risks and unknowns.
20 Describing the Guards in this way allowed the German authorities to silence the Italian fears of Germanization of the

The Civic Guards were closely interconnected with the M.D.T. Regiments, carrying out the same functions of supervision and control of the territory foreseen for the M.D.T. and, indeed, in some cases, going to overlap their skills.

Trieste's Civic Guard

At the end of 1943, the conviction spread among the Trieste authorities that part of the Friulian territory could be annexed to Austria. Alongside this hypothetical risk, there was a more concrete one, that is, the occupation of the city by the Titian partisans. It was this context of uncertainty and danger that prompted the Podestà of Trieste Cesare Pagnini to negotiate with the German military authorities the establishment of an armed department placed under his direct dependence. At first the Germans proved to be refractory to this initiative, much preferring the establishment of a military unit to be included in the Polizei row of SS. The Podestà Pagnini was not intimidated and continued undaunted in the realization of this project and, finally, on 11th January 1944 the announcement of enlistment for the so-called "Civic Guard", an armed body that had to guarantee public order, preserving the city from any military and political threat. Enrollment was to take place on a voluntary basis (initially open to classes from 1920 to 1924, it was soon extended to previous classes) and the aspiring Guards should have, in the intentions of the Podestà, had love and faith towards the Homeland. The body's duties were city security, air and fire protection; the flag was that of the Municipality of Trieste, given that the Italian one had been banned in the city by the Germanic authorities on 11 November 1943. The Guard subsequently took part also in actions to repress the partisan phenomenon on the Karst and also took care of searching for the renitents to the draft and the employment service for the Germans.

The announcement was a success immediately, about fifty officers and non-commissioned officers of the dissolved Royal Army immediately joined; when fully operational, the Guard reached the number of 1,600 men, organized on two Battalions and two anti-aircraft batteries. The Germans, however, managed to exercise close and direct control over the Civic Guard, through the general of the SS Von Malsen and Colonel Temtet and also the official name of the department, according to the German authorities, was however "Stadtschutz Triest". It was even imposed that the training should be conducted by German SS and Polizei instructors[21], commanded by General Erasmus von Malsen, an attempt was also made to dress the body in SS uniforms. These were however categorically rejected by the Guards and Pagnini managed to equip the body with its own uniform in gray-green cloth with a peculiar cut, made by the Beltrami company[22]. The same factory also made a summer uniform similar to the winter one in khaki cotton. The uniform was completed with amaranth-colored rhomboid insignia with the silver halberd, symbol of the city of Trieste. Courses began in February 1944; they lasted 40 days each and the first course, made up of the ranks of the Royal Army who had answered the call immediately, was held at the elementary schools in via Combi. From this first round the coordinators came out who, later, supported by German non-commissioned officers, trained all the other volunteers.

O.Z.A.K. and to make these departments appear as autonomous units and not related to the interests of the Reich.
21 The officers followed a special course held by the SS in Duino (TS).
22 At first, all that could be done was to draw on the warehouses of the dissolved Royal Army to equip the soldiers, waiting for a specific uniform. Even when the peculiar uniform of the unit was adopted, the aspirants used the gray army fatigue uniform of the Royal Army during the training courses. With the passing of the months, however, the difficult war economy imposed the recovery of the "recoverable", leaving the discretion of the kit to the personal initiative, which continued to maintain the distinctive sign of the red badges with the Halberd symbol of Trieste.

The first activity carried out by the Guard was the recovery of the weapons abandoned by the Carabinieri and by the Guardia di Finanza, weapons that allowed to improve the unit's equipment[23].

After knowing that the oath had to be signed in both Italian and German, some official students of the Guardi Civica proved recalcitrant and were therefore summoned to the Command of General Globocnik, who warned them that he would consider enemies all those who had not signed[24]. On 13th May the body of the Civic Guard officially assumed roles, grades and duties, effectively entering into effective service[25].

Trieste was hit hard by an allied bombing on June 10th, 1944 and the soldiers of the Guard were employed in the pitiful relief work for the population and, following this attack, numerous detachments were organized, to guard the strategic points of the Friuli capital and on the 25th July the Guard occupied all the Carabinieri Stations outside the city, before they ended up under the control of German Polizei. Detachments were also placed along the railway lines, often controlled by mixed patrols, composed of civic guards and German soldiers unsuitable for first-line activity.

Following the occupation of the weapon stations and the establishment of the garrisons located around the city, the Guard took on this structure[26]:

- Commander-in-Chief: Colonel Cesare Pagnini[27]
- Effective Military Commander: Captain Giulio Motka
- Major Assistant: Lieutenant Steno Pirnetti
- Administration: Captain Raimondo Marpugo then Lieutenant Ettore Franchi
- Enrollment: Colonel Renato Duse
- 1st Battalion (Trieste – Podgora barracks with 15 detachments):
  - 1st Company
  - 2nd Company
  - 3rd Company
  - 4th Company
- 2nd Battalion (Trieste – Primary schools in via San Giorgio):
  - 5th Company
  - 6th Company
  - 7th Company
  - 8th Company

---

23 A part of these weapons were secretly hidden by both pro-fascist elements and elements close to the resistance movement, in order to be used in future moments of need.

24 According to the testimony of the official student Bruno Steffè, only he and three other students definitively refused to sign the oath formula thus conceived.

25 The text of the oath of the Civic Guard was in fact bilingual and was first recited in German, a sign of the subordination of the Corps to the Germanic authorities. The complete text said: "Conscious of my duty, postomes of my will, I swear before God, the Almighty, to unconditionally obey the orders of my superiors and to take up arms against the enemies of my homeland and to fight with fidelity and courage in training under German directives. I am ready to leave my life for this fight. So be it and God help me!". Some official students of the Guardia Civica proved reluctant to take this oath, after knowing that it had to be signed in both Italian and German. They were therefore summoned to the Command of General Globocnik, who warned him that he would consider enemies who had not signed.

26 Organization chart referred to July 25th, 1944.

27 The Podestà Pagnini had this assignment (and the relative military rank) for honorary purposes only, in fact not exercising any effective command.

The second Battalion will subsequently be dissolved by order of the German Command and many staff will be destined for compulsory labor units.

Over the months some Civic Guards, by personal decision, began to clandestinely support the activity of the Resistance. Forming small groups of partisan resistance within the Guard, they secretly took possession of weapons that attempted to pass to the armed groups of the Volunteer Corps for Freedom, but many of them were discovered and arrested by the Germans and passed for weapons or interned in San Sabba.

The relations between the Trieste Civic Guard and the Republican Fascist Party were rather tense, above all because of the total independence of the city's militia precisely from the Party. Even relations with the partisan forces were based on distrust, since the Guard was considered a pro-fascist militia. In reality it is not possible to place exactly the position of unity created by Podestà Pagnini in the varied universe of the republican departments: if on the one hand there was certainly a current inside the Guard that, as we have seen, supported the Resistance, albeit in an illegal way, on the other hand, it is indisputable that the Guard itself was employed in repressive activities.

In late 1944, about 200 "Vigili"[28] of the Guardia were forcibly disarmed and sent by the German authorities to dig trenches above Trieste and near Fiume, since an allied landing in Istria was feared; only in January of the following year did the Brigade return to their ranks.

In April 1944 the Civic Guard of Trieste, which had come to have more than 30 detachments and a staff of about 1,650 men, had this structure:

- Commander-in-Chief: Colonel Cesare Pagnini
- Effective Military Commander: Major Giacomo Juraga
- Major Assistant: Lieutenant Aldo Cucchi
- Command Office: Sergeant Alfonso Fabricci
- Administration Service: Lieutenant Ettore Franchi
- Health Service: Medical Lieutenant Guido Parini
- Propaganda Office: Second Lieutenant Mario Righi
- Command Company: Lieutenants Clescovich, Nemaz, Cucchi
- Company of the Guard: Lieutenant Steno Pirnetti
- 1st Battalion (Trieste – Podgora barracks with 15 detachments):
    - 1st Company
    - 2nd Company
    - 3rd Company
    - 4th Company
- Anti-tank Support
- Anti-Aircraft Artillery Group:
    - 1st Battery (Opicina)
    - 2nd Battery (Albano Vescovà)

In the last days of the war, the Civic Guard of Trieste engaged with other Italian units in the area to prevent any act of sabotage of the port structures by the Germans. At 5.30 on April 30, 1945, the general alarm signal was given with the sirens of the city, signaling the beginning of the insurrection. The Municipality of Trieste was placed under the garrison of about twenty

---
28 This is the name used to indicate the soldiers of Trieste's Civic Guard.

Vigils under the command of Lieutenant Pirnetti: a large tricolor was hoisted (for the first time since the Germans had prohibited its use in the city) and a city flag with the symbol dell'alabarda. The external principals received orders to return to the city, but the return was made difficult due to the gunfights that were taking place between the Germans and the first slave units; several times the latter unsuccessfully ordered the Guards to lay down their arms and surrender. German soldiers repeatedly tried to convince the garrison of the Town Hall to abandon the town hall, but the Brigade responded every time strenuously shooting with all their weapons. The resistance of the barricaded Guards lasted until noon, when news of the imminent arrival of the Allies came; after a few hours, in fact, the New Zealand avant-gardes entered the city. The will to preserve the city from the Slavic intrusiveness was lacking, as was instead wished by the authorities of the Social Republic, and no agreement was reached thanks to which the republican forces would have guaranteed the Italian spirit of Trieste: the Prefect and the Podestà proposed to keep the Civic Guard in arms at the disposal of the CLN club to ensure public order, but the proposal was categorically rejected. At 19, therefore, the Podestà Pagnini handed over the city in the hands of Professor Giovanni Paladin, representative of the C.L.N., effectively leaving the Titini free field. Shortly before, the Civic Guard, deployed in the reception hall of the town hall, had received signs of recognition for the sacrifice made in those confused days, during which 2 policemen had perished and no less than 8 had been injured. In the meantime, the city had been occupied by the Slav partisans, who immediately dissolved the National Liberation Committee by force and forced the Guard to surrender. Thus, began the sad forty days of Yugoslav occupation of the city of Trieste, during which many policemen were sought after by Titian partisans, arrested and interned in prison camps, where most of them were eliminated or perished due to the hardships suffered. At the end of December 11 Brigade were tried, sentenced as war criminals and shot in Ljubljana.

The Corps of the Civic Guard of Trieste had a total of 112 casualties, of which at least 6 were inflicted by the partisans of Tito in Basovizza[29], and 28 between wounded and maimed. Five officers and a dozen soldiers, who, as we have seen, supported the resistance movement, were deported to Germany and only a few returned.

Gorizia's Civic Guard

In the Gorizia's unit, the agents of the Municipal Police were enrolled, who had proved unable to counteract the partisans' activities. The Civic Guard of Gorizia, contrary to similar units that arose in the rest of Istria, also enlisted soldiers of Slavic origin, following the pressure of the Germans, who aimed, in this way, to diminish the Italianness of the Guard and to humiliate, to consequently, the Italians residing in the area. The choice to place a German officer in command of the unit went in the same direction, so much so that the spirit of the unit was undermined and, with the passage of time, the aim of maintaining the Italian spirit of Gorizia was lost. Composed of about 250 elements, the Civic Guard of Gorizia had Captain Giordano Cumar, Gorizia as deputy commander; there were more than 20 casualties ascertained, but it is plausible that, in reality, they were more than double. Recent research has ascertained the names of 5 of the perished Guards. One of these was captured near Biglia di Gorizia on November 29th, 1944 together with 6 other comrades whose name is unknown. The 7 soldiers

---

[29] A total of 21 Guards were arrested by the communist partisans in May 1945 who never returned; a group of Civic Guards was killed near Duino by German soldiers in 1944 and others perished during the partisan insurrection, by German hand.

were then led to Ranziano, where they were passed through the arms by the Slavs.

On April 30th, 1945, German troops withdrew from Gorizia and the Civic Guard formed armed teams, together with police officers from the local police station, the Carabinieri, civilians and even some pro-Italian local partisans.

These teams, which were supposed to take control of the city pending the arrival of the Allies, sustained gunfights when the Chetniks arrived trying to enter Gorizia. During the fighting, a non-commissioned officer of the dissolved Royal Italian Army, who was involved in the C.L.N., advised the soldiers and public security agents to leave the city, to avoid problems with the Yugoslav partisans, now on the outskirts of Gorizia. Most of the military, however, remained in their positions, convinced that they had only done their duty. Many of them were arrested and deported by the Yugoslav partisans of the IX Corpus in the following days; few escaped death during detention.

The unit was equipped with only individual weapons (Beretta model 34 and 35 pistols, muskets model 91 and some MAB38) and light squad weapons (Breda 30 submachine guns).

Koper's Civic Guards

The birth of the Civic Guard in Capodistria (the current Koper) can be traced back to the announcement that appeared on 11 March 1944[30] on the walls of the city, notice announcing the birth of the "Territorial Reserve Guard". Although the announcement was signed by the Prefect Commissioner Mario De Vilos and urged voluntary enrollment in the newly formed corps of all the valid men of the town, the initiative was entirely German, so much so that the body also had the Germanic name of "Landschutz"[31]. The purpose of these units, as we have seen, was to recruit personnel to be assigned to defend urban centers, removing them from the partisan attraction. Theoretically, the German authorities should have provided light armor for the unit and paid for the enlisted. Membership was high (after all, joining the Guard was a fairly simple way to escape forced enlistment by both partisan, German and Fascist sides) and 4 Platoons and a Service Team were thus created, with a total staff of about 350 men, 6 acting officers. The armament provided initially was very scarce, about fifty 98/38 model rifles, a thousand cartridges, a MAB, twenty hand grenades; even the clothing delivered to the Guard was insufficient: it was in fact a dozen gray-green cloth coats. However, in addition to a green identification badge, a red bracelet with the coat of arms of Istria and the body name in Italian and German was distributed to all. The Guardia was based in the Palazzo della Loggia; the first commander was Dr. Antonio Padovan, former Captain of the Royal Army, to which was succeeded very early by Lieutenant Paolo Paulin, elementary teacher, who, in disagreement with the fascist and German authorities, had to leave the command, enlisting in the X MAS stationed in Pula, to Lieutenant Bruno Busan, promoted to Captain. Aldo Cherin

---

30 In reality there was a precedent in Koper: in the Trieste daily newspaper "Il Piccolo" of November 14th, 1943 an article entitled "The Civic Guard established in Koper" is found. The day before, a demonstration was held in the central square of the city in support of the Republican Armed Forces, with the aim of encouraging the voluntarism of the inhabitants of the area. It is probable that on this occasion the foundations were laid for the establishment of the Koper Civic Guard. Nominally it had a staff of 350 men and was in command of Paolo Almerigogna, in support of a Public Health Committee, formed in those convulsive days. This Guard was short-lived and was dissolved after only a few days.

31 This denomination appears to be in contradiction with the citizen character of the Guard of Koper: "Landschutz" is a term that refers to a territorial defense unit, with tasks extended to a very large territory, certainly not limited to a city and its areas nearby. In this case the correct denomination would be, as for the Civic Guard of Trieste, "Stadtschutz".

and Lauro Ghitter, former Lieutenants of the Army before the Armistice, were assigned the task of Helpers, as well as other officers of the dissolved Royal Army assumed the function of inspection officers. Training in arms and behavior in service was given in the main courtyard of the convent of Santa Chiara. The guard service was carried out by 4 patrols of 3 men each, from sunset, until dawn; the main task of the patrols was to control the blackout and curfew. Other men were posted in two fixed guard posts (one on the Almerigogna Fund and one on the Calda Fund) and a sighting service, consisting of two men, watched from the bell tower of the cathedral, to signal the arrival of isolated planes, which could strafe at low altitude. A dozen soldiers were later sent to garrison the bridge over the River Risano, the target of partisan sabotage, together with some plainclothes Finance Guards. The Guard of Koper also organized a dormitory shelter at its headquarters for travelers surprised by the curfew, who could thus find hospitality for the night. The Territorial Reserve Guard absorbed the Auxiliary Militia of the M.D.T., since they performed the same tasks[32]. The Guard was frowned upon by members of the Republican Fascist Party, with whom he initially shared the patrol service; however, it should be noted that, as will be discovered in the days of the partisan insurrection, a group of militants, including the commander Busan himself, had forged relationships with the clandestine National Liberation Committee. This interaction was so strong as to prompt the Prefectural Commissioner, in early April, to try to convince Captain Bruno Busan to act as an intermediary at the C.L.N. for an orderly handover of powers by the fascist authorities, unfortunately without success. Fearing that the Germans could make the mines that had placed in the city port shine, Koper was alarmed starting at 11 p.m. on April 27th. On the morning of the 28th the Germans withdrew their more advanced garrisons, including that of the Risano bridge; the detachment of the Guard, commanded by Aldo Cherini, took note of the situation, thus discovering that in the cantonal house the Germanic soldiers had abandoned much material in the haste to flee. The detachment, in order not to remain isolated, put in place the retreat plan to the city, which has already been planned for days. With the help of a fisherman, the men were embarked at the mouth of the Risano river, thus avoiding the folding overland, which could have been dangerous because of the first partisan bands that were moving. In the night between 28th and 29th April the local garrison of the M.D.T. broke up, abandoning weapons and materials, after the detachment of Buje had returned to the city. A small column of the Militia thus took the road to Trieste and some officers and soldiers asked to have civilian clothes at the Command of the Guard at the Lodge; the last group of legionnaires left Koper on board a truck at dawn. On the morning of April 29th, the Territorial Guard thus found itself to be the only Italian body organized to defend the city, together with some Carabinieri and a few Guardia di Finanza. The Guard therefore organized itself to guarantee public order, staking the post office, the headquarters of the Istrian Savings Bank, the shipyard, the public offices and the food warehouses. Many of the weapons abandoned by the fleeing Militia were recovered by the Guard and deposited with the Command at the Lodge. It was not possible to rake all the abandoned weapons, because some elements, which secretly supported the Titian partisans, managed to steal a part out of town. On April 29th the provincial road that led to Trieste was cluttered by the German autocolumns that were folding from Pula to the Friuli capital and their presence was sufficient to keep the Slav

---

32 The Auxiliary Militia Corps was created in December 1943 within the 2nd Territorial Defense Militia Regiment; it was composed of militarized civilians, but without uniforms, and carried out tasks of an internal order, identical to those entrusted subsequently to the "Landschutz".

partisans away from Koper. In the town, the inhabitants hoped for an imminent arrival of the Anglo-American troops, the members of the C.L.N. local instead they waited, in vain, for the arrival of an Italian military formation, while Titian supporters yearned for a rapid regime change. Around 13.00 the German batteries of Punta Grossa began a weak bombing of the city, believing it already occupied by the partisans. The cannon fire, despite having lasted for many hours, did not cause casualties.

The last German detachment in the city, that of the port, was approached by a representative of the C.L.N., accompanied by the Captain of the Guard Bruno Busan, who, as we have seen, had established clandestine relations with the Committee. The German commander refused the partisans' surrender proposals, assuring however that he would remove his men from Koper and, if not threatened, that he would not make the mines of the port shine. However, Captain Busan had a security service set up, so that timely action could be taken to avoid the explosion of the mines. On the morning of April 30th around 4 o'clock in the morning, the Germans left Koper on board the steamer "Italy", which they had seized earlier, and on which the last legionaries who were late for the Militia had hastily embarked. The future of the Territorial Reserve Guard was already marked when he intervened for the last time shortly after the departure of the German soldiers, to disperse a group of supporters of the Slavic communist movement that had concentrated outside the Porta della Muda, after raking the weapons abandoned in the city. The Slav partisans occupied the city a few hours later; the Territorial Reserve Guard was tolerated by the titine authorities only for a few days, only to be released by force.

Pordenone's Civic Guard

Unfortunately, there is very little information found on the last of the four Civic Guard units, the one of Pordenone. We only know that it was organized in 1944, it was commanded by the Lieutenant Pietro Colombo and the deputy commander was the Lieutenant Mario Zagnis.

COMUNE DI TRIESTE

COSTITUZIONE DI UNA GUARDIA CIVICA

Concittadini!

Il disorientamento e la disgregazione di questi ultimi mesi, la sorte toccata recentemente a città a noi particolarmente care ci hanno dato il triste insegnamento che soltanto le collettività che sanno difendersi combattendo hanno sicurezza di vita.

Per garantire l'ordine e l'intangibilità della nostra Trieste da qualsiasi minaccia, ho deciso di istituire, alla mia diretta ed esclusiva dipendenza, la guardia civica, che dovrà essere composta dai giovani migliori, i quali, pur nel disordine generale, hanno conservata immutata la fede nella Patria e nella saldezza della gente di questa nostra regione.

Ad essi mi rivolgo, da italiano ad italiani, da fratello a fratelli e commetto nelle loro mani la vita dei cittadini, l'onore della città e un simbolo incontaminato: l'alabarda di S. Sergio.

Ispirato a questi principi, che discendono dalle nostre più pure tradizioni, il Corpo, al quale vi chiamo, non può che avere a base un carattere volontaristico ed il proposito di assolvere un altissimo dovere civico. Per tal motivo ritengo che non debba costituire un'attività esclusiva, ma compatibile, sia pure con qualche limitazione, con le ordinarie occupazioni di tutti coloro che, avendone i requisiti, sentiranno il bisogno e l'orgoglio di assolverla.

Le domande di arruolamento, stese su moduli forniti dall'Amministrazione, saranno accolte nei giorni feriali dal 15 al 22 del corrente mese, dalle ore 9 alle ore 12 e dalle ore 15.30 alle ore 17.30, nella sala della Consulta al I. piano del Palazzo municipale (ingresso dal portone n. 1 di via Procureria).

Le assegnazioni ai vari gradi e la fissazione degli assegni saranno da me disposte dopo raccolte ed esaminate le domande di arruolamento.

Per essere arruolati occorrono i seguenti requisiti:

1) **appartenere alle classi dal 1900 al 1926;**
2) **essere incensurati;**
3) **essere fermamente risoluti ad operare per la salvezza e l'onore della città.**

Dal Palazzo di città, 11 gennaio 1944 - XXII

IL PODESTA'
avv. CESARE PAGNINI

▲ Poster that announces the formation of the Trieste's Civic Guard and calls citizens to join it.

▲ Soldiers of the Civic Guard of Trieste during the training course; all students wear the fatigued uniform of the dissolved Royal Army.

▼ A group of soldiers of the Trieste's Civic Guard parades in front of the chief of the Polizei of Trieste, General von Malsen on August 12th, 1944 (Adria Illustrierte).

▲ Civic Guard's soldiers employed in the rescue work to the civilian population, after the allied bombing that hit Trieste on 10th June 1944.

▲ A soldier of the Trieste Guard in ordinary winter uniform between the SS- Brigadeführer Erasmus von Malsen and the Podestà of Trieste Cesare Pagnini (Arena).

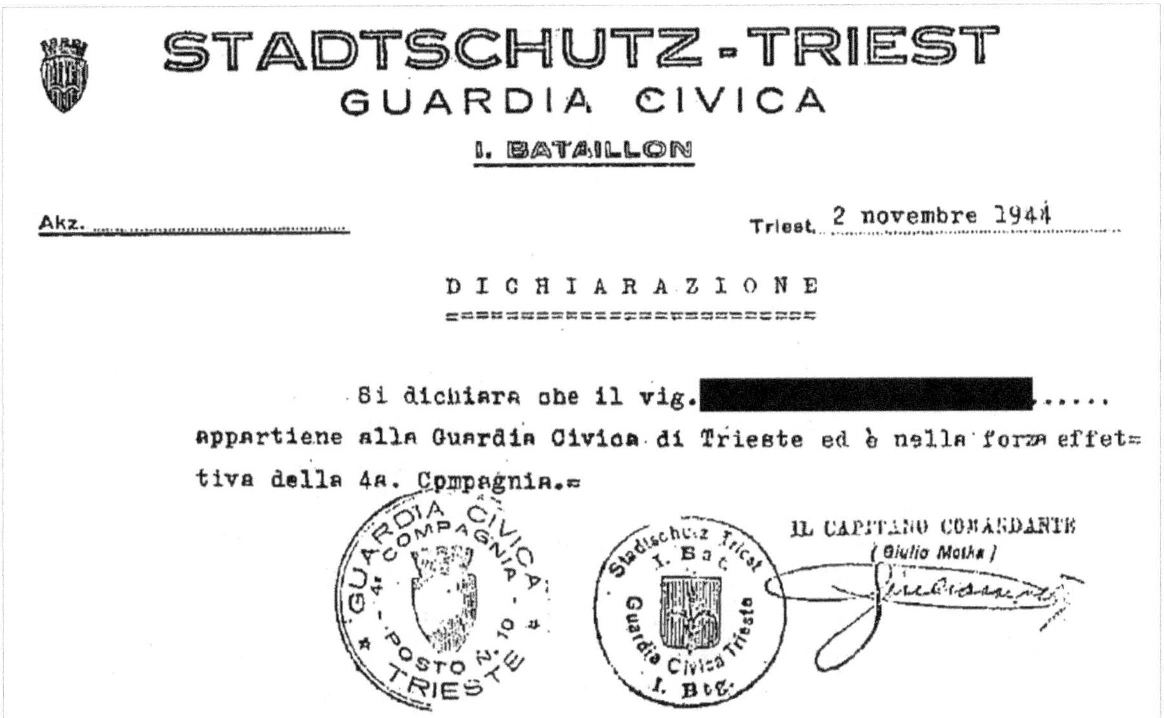

STADTSCHUTZ - TRIEST
GUARDIA CIVICA
I. BATAILLON

Akz. _____   Triest, 2 novembre 1944

DICHIARAZIONE

Si dichiara che il vig. ███████████
appartiene alla Guardia Civica di Trieste ed è nella forza effet=
tiva della 4a. Compagnia.=

IL CAPITANO COMANDANTE
(Giulio Moska)

▲ Document certifying the service in the Civic Guard of Trieste of a "Vigile" (the members of the Guard were called "Policemen"). The document is very interesting, because it reports the header in German and Italian and bears the bilingual stamps of the 4th Company of the 1st Battalion and the 1st Battalion itself, in addition to the signature of the Company Commander, Captain Moska.

▼ Group of Guards and Graduates; a soldier wears an out of ordinance Italian camouflage jacket.

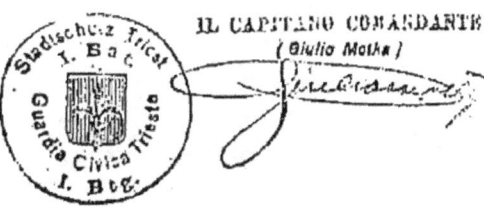

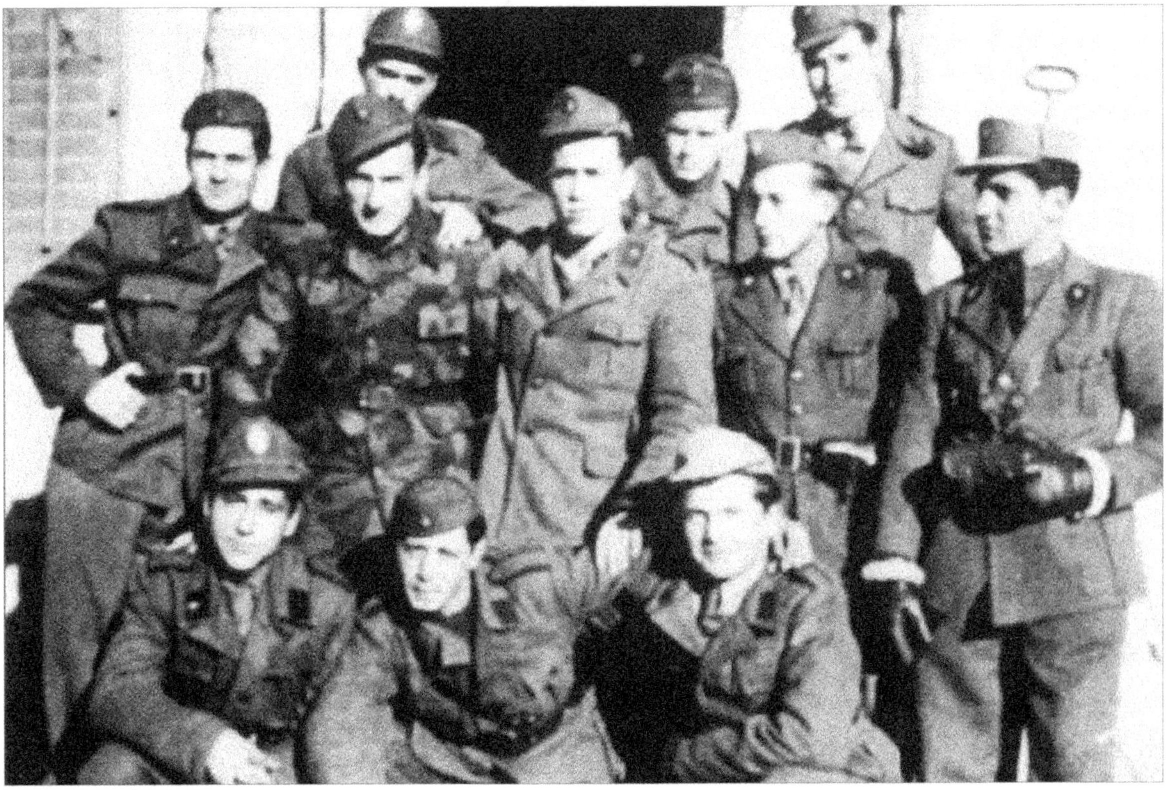

COMUNE DI TRIESTE

GUARDIA CIVICA
STADTSCHUTZ TRIEST
GUARDIA CIVICA TRIESTE
Comando 1ª Compagnia

(1)

RUOLINO TASCABILE

DELLA

FORZA DEL SUINDICATO REPARTO

Copia tenuta dal (2)

(1) Compagnia
(2) Comandante di compagnia o subalterno

LA EDITORIALE LIBRARIA S. A.
TRIESTE

▲ Pocket ID document of the 1st Company of the Civic Guard of Trieste.

▲ Guard in winter clothes in Trieste during a patrol.

▲ Image taken during an exhibition held in Trieste dedicated to the Civic Guard in 1994; on the left the uniform of a Marshal of the Trieste's Guard, on the right, with the unit's flag, a "Vigile" with a model 40 jacket already of the Royal Army, readapted for use for the Civic Guard.

▼ Model 42 cap in gray-green cloth of the Civic Guard of Trieste; the metal frieze bears the coat of arms of the city and was already used by the Triestine Municipal Guards before the war (Cucut).

▲ Insignia of the Trieste Guard: the bottom is crimson, while the thread and the halberd are in silver thread (Cucut).

▼ The plaque dedicated to the fallen of the Civic Guard in Trieste, erected by the citizens in 2005, sixty years after the end of the second world war, and several times stupidly damaged by vandals.

▲ Souvenir medal awarded to veterans of the Civic Guard of Trieste. The ribbon is red with a white insert and recalls the colors of the Julian city (Crippa Collection).

▲ Ceremony held in Koper on November 14, 1943, in the central square of the city, in support of voluntary membership of the Republican Armed Forces. It was the first occasion when we talked about Koper's Civic Guard. In the background the town Loggia, which will later be the headquarters of the Guard. The armored vehicles and trucks are of the "Mazza di Ferro" Company of what will be the 1st Territorial Defense Militia Regiment (MNZ).

BIBLIOGRAPHY

Books

• Arena Nino, "Soli contro tutti", Edizioni Ultima Crociata, Milano, 1993

• Arena Nino, "L'Italia in guerra 1940/45", Ermanno Albertelli Editore, Parma, 1997.

• Arena Nino, "R.S.I. – Forze Armate della Repubblica Sociale – La guerra in Italia – 1943 – 1944 – 1945", Ermanno Albertelli Editore, Parma, 2002.

• AA.VV., "Storia della Guardia Civica di Trieste 1944-1994", Associazione Guardia Civica, Trieste, 1994

• Bigai Diego, "La Guardia Civica di Trieste" in "Guerra Civile" numero 3, Editrice Il Veliero, Imperia.

• Cerceo Vincenzo, "Stadtschutz – La Guardia Civica di Trieste nel 1944 – 1945", supplemento al numero 163 – gennaio 2003 di "La nuova Alabarda e la Coda del Diavolo", Trieste, 2003.

• Cherini Aldo, "La Guardia Territoriale di Capodistria, marzo 1944 – maggio 1945", autoedizione del 1992 (ristampa maggio 2011).

• Chiussi Tommaso, Di Giusto Stefano, "Globocnik's Men in Italy, 1943-45: Abteilung R and the SS-Wachmannschaften of the Operationszone Adriatisches Küstenland", Schiffer Military History, Atglen, Pennsylvania, U.S.A., 2016.

• Colummi Cristiana, Ferrari Liliana, Nassisi Gianni, Trani Giorgio, "Storia di un esodo – Istria 1945 – 1956", Istituto Regionale per il movimento di Liberazione nel Friuli-Venezia Giulia, Trieste, 1980.

• Corbatti Sergio, Nava Marco, "...come il diamante!", Laran Editions, Bruxelles 2008.

• Crippa Paolo, "I reparti corazzati della R.S.I. 1943 – 1945", Marvia Edizioni, Voghera (PV), 2006.

• Crippa Paolo, "Italia 43 – 45 – I blindati di circostanza della Guerra Civile", Mattioli 1885, Parma, 2014.

• Crippa Paolo, "I mezzi corazzati della Guerra Civile 43 -45", Mattioli 1885, Parma, 2015.

• Crippa Paolo, Cucut Carlo, "I reparti corazzati italiani nei Balcani 1941 – 1945", Luca Cristini Editore, Zanica (BG), 2019.

• Corbanese Girolamo, Mansutti Aldo, "Storia d'Italia. Zona di Operazioni del Litorale Adriatico. I Protagonisti (settembre 1943 – maggio 1945)", Aviani & Aviani Editori, Udine, 2008.

• Cucut Carlo, "Le Forze Armate della R.S.I. 1943 – 1945 – Forze di Terra", G.M.T., Trento, 2005.

- Cucut Carlo, "Le Forze Armate della R.S.I. sul confine orientale – settembre 1943 – maggio 1945", Marvia Edizioni, Voghera (PV), 2009.

- Dalcich Torquato (pseudonimo di Aldo Quattrocchi). "Un diario (1944 – 1945), autoedizione, Firenze, 1987.

- De Ferra Claudio, "Un milione e 1", Edizioni Nuovo Fronte, 2001.

- Di Giusto Stefano, "I reparti Panzer nell'Operationszone Adriatisches Kustenland", Edizioni della Laguna, Mariano del Friuli (GO), 2002.

- Di Giusto Stefano, "Operationszone Adriatisches Kustenland. Udine Gorizia Trieste Pola Fiume e Lubiana durante l'occupazione tedesca 1943 - 1945", I.F.S.M.L., Udine, 2005.

- Giusti Maria Teresa, Rossi Aga, "Una guerra a parte. I militari italiani nei Balcani, 1940-1945", Il Mulino, Bologna, 2017.

- Guglielmi Daniele, Tallillo Andrea, Tallillo Antonio, "CarriL3. Carri Veloci, Carri leggeri, derivati", G.M.T., Trento, 2004.

- Kuchler Heinz, "Fregi, mostrine e distintivi della R.S.I.", Intergest, Milano, 1974.

- Marzetti Paolo, " Uniformi e distintivi italiani 1933 – 1945", Ermanno Albertelli Editore, Parma 1995.

- Oliva Gianni, "Foibe – Le stragi negate degli italiani della Venezia Giulia e dell'Istria", Arnoldo Mondadori Editore, Milano, 2002.

- Papo da Montona Luigi, "L'ultima bandiera. Storia del Reggimento Istria", Edizioni T.E.R., 2000.

- Pisanò Giorgio, "Gli ultimi in grigioverde", Edizioni F.P.E., Milano 1967.

- Pisanò Giorgio, "Storia della Guerra Civile in Italia", Edizioni F.P.E., Milano 1967.

- Predoević Dinko, Dimitrijević Bojan, "Oklopne postrojbe Sila Osovine na jugoistoku Europe u Drugome svjetskom ratu", Despot Infinitus d.o.o., Zagabria (Croazia), 2015.

- Roberti Giorgio, "Con fegato sano a mala guerra. Guastatori alpini genieri e Legionari della R.S.I.", Edizioni Nuovo Fronte,

- Rosignoli Guido, "R.S.I. Uniformi, distintivi, equipaggiamenti e armi 1943-45", Ermanno Albertelli Editore, Parma, 1998.

- Rustia Giorgio, "Reggimenti Milizia Difesa Territoriale – Atti, meriti e sacrifici dei Regimenti Milizia Difesa Territoriale al confine orientale italiano", Aviani & Aviani Editori, Udine, 2011.

• Sparacino Fausto, "Distintivi e medaglie della R.S.I." E.M.I., Milano, 1994.

• Sparacino Fausto, "Distintivi e medaglie della R.S.I., della Legione S.S. Italiana, dei Veterani della R.S.I." E.M.I., Milano, 1998.

Quotidiani, riviste e periodici

• "Acta" della Fondazione R.S.I. – Istituto Storico, Terranuova Bracciolini (AR), numeri vari.

• "Adria Illustrierte", numeri vari.

• "Il Piccolo", quotidiano di Trieste, numeri vari.

• "L'Arena di Pola", periodico in lingua italiana di Pola, numeri vari.

Various pubblications

• Opuscolo della mostra "Guardia Civica di Trieste 1944 – 1945", edito a cura del Centro Regionale Studi di Storia Militare Antica e Moderna, Trieste, 1994.

• Opuscolo della mostra "Trieste 1945 - Prima e dopo 1943 - 1947", edito a cura del Centro Regionale Studi di Storia Militare Antica e Moderna, Trieste, 1995.

Other documents

• "Situazione dell'Istria centrale e meridionale – Estratto della relazione dell'Ufficiale M.U. in servizio presso presidi dell'Istria", 10 luglio 1944, copia fotostatica in possesso degli autori.

• "Relazione sulla situazione in Istria", senza data, copia fotostatica in possesso degli autori.

• "Rapportino sulla situazione partigiani n°1", 1° Gennaio 1945, copia fotostatica in possesso degli autori.

TITOLI GIÀ PUBBLICATI
TITLES ALREADY PUBLISHING

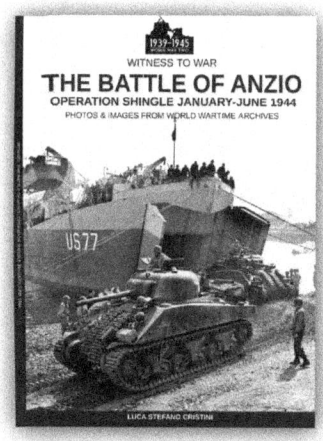

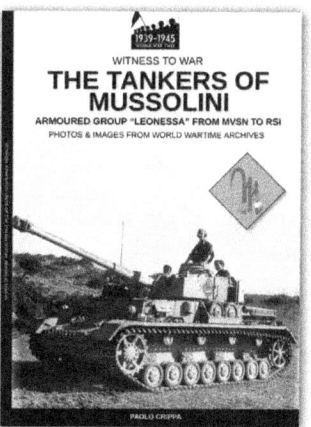
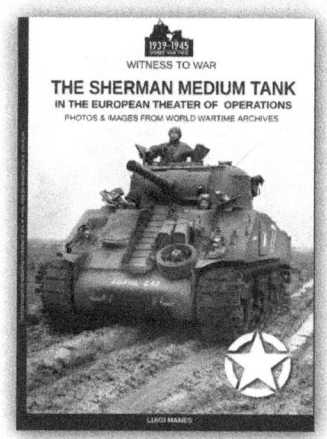

BOOKS TO COLLECT

www.ingramcontent.com/pod-product-compliance
Lightning Source LLC
LaVergne TN
LVHW081545070526
838199LV00057B/3778